Breathe

Breathe

Breathe
Reflect
Empathize
Accept
Thank
Hearten
Engage

Maxine Swisa

Printed in the United States of America
ISBN: 0989366219
ISBN 13: 9780989366212
Library of Congress Control Number: 2017909739
Inspiration Education Press, Santa Fe, NM

This book is lovingly dedicated to my daughters, Maya and Adi, who remind me to breathe, reflect, empathize, accept, thank, hearten, engage, and understand every day.

Acknowledgments

I express my deepest gratitude to four people who have been helpful, supportive, and loving throughout the creation of this book. First, I thank my friend and coheart, Kristine Menn. Kristine and I became friends on the first day of graduate school and our friendship has blossomed ever since. The concept of BREATHE originated during the summer of 2014 as Kristine and I prepared a joint presentation for the Sandanona Conference at SIT Graduate Institute. I did not know at that time that it would turn into the basis for this book as a reflection of my life's work.

Next, I would like to express my gratitude to Susan Barduhn, retired professor, SIT Graduate Institute. She offered me guidance and encouragement throughout my studies at SIT Graduate Institute. Her insights helped me grow personally and professionally.

I thank my dear friend and colleague, Jenny Lake Sanborn. Jenny and I spent hours walking and talking about this book and life. She helped me work through many of the activities, including the gratitude mobile, the human knot, the yarn activity, and others. I'm saddened to say that Jenny Lake Sanborn passed away on September 29, 2016. I am grateful and honored to have been her friend. May her memory be a blessing to those who knew her and loved her.

Last, I am deeply grateful to my close friend and business partner, Marya Corneli. Her editing help during the final stages of this book has been a tremendous gift. Marya is my daily source of inspiration, humor, and loving-kindness. Together, we are creating our vision for the future through *inspirationeducation.us,* committed to uplifting our potential through mind/body education, compassion training, and creativity.

I also thank some of the better-known thought leaders and spiritual teachers who have inspired me over the years. I have had the good fortune to meet many of them and participate in seminars with them.

First, I thank Deepak Chopra for his ability to share complex ideas and concepts in an accessible way. Reading *The Seven Spiritual Laws of Success* was my initiation into exploring the world of infinite possibilities.

I also thank the late Wayne Dyer. His courage and willingness to share his human frailties with humor and wisdom was, and still is, a source of encouragement to me.

The first time I heard the word "mindfulness" was reading Jon Kabat-Zinn's book, *Wherever You Go, There You Are.* This book introduced me to several meditation techniques as well.

Dan Siegel's meditation, the wheel of awareness, as well as his scientific exploration of neuroplasticity have changed the way I experience learning, meditation, and my ability to integrate the brain/mind/body connection.

I also thank Sharon Salzberg for making her lovingkindness meditation so readily available to all of us. My heart opens a little more each time I meditate on loving-kindness.

We are so fortunate to live during a time when we can listen and learn from His Holiness the Dalai Lama. His ability to transcend religion and encourage compassion is a gift to all humanity.

I am filled with gratitude to Joe Dispenza for his dedicated, dynamic presence. His passion and love for life is truly inspiring. Thanks to Joe's scientific explanations about our power to heal and generate the future we want for ourselves, I am even more excited about the infinite possibilities that lie ahead.

Gratitude, kindness, love, and compassion have become part of my daily practice. It is not always easy, especially when life throws me curveballs. In spite of challenges that arise, I know I am happier, healthier, and more mindful as a result of integrating these positive emotions in my life.

I am extremely grateful for all the people who have been my guides throughout my spiritual journey.

Preface

BREATHE is an acronym for Breathe, Reflect, Empathize, Accept, Thank, Hearten, Engage. Using these skills allows for a holistic approach to living a healthy and balanced life personally and professionally. This book took form as a result of my personal spiritual journey and my professional experience. When training and teaching, I noticed that the majority of participants enjoyed experiential activities that included time and space for self-reflection, relaxation, and meditation. I began looking for books, seminars, and workshops that explored these areas. Deepak Chopra, Jon Kabat-Zinn, Dan Siegel, Eckhart Tolle, et al. offer insights into the benefits of meditation and mindfulness as a vehicle for improved quality of life. His Holiness the Dalai Lama describes compassion as a basic human value that is separate from religious practices and beliefs. The positive effects of gratitude on a person's well-being have been studied by Dr. Robert Emmons and others. Charles A. Curran has written about the importance of understanding and its connection to our sense of belonging. SIT Graduate Institute's focus on reflective teaching practices provides another important aspect for leading a fulfilling life that incorporates a holistic approach to lifelong learning. Each chapter includes practical activities to use in the workplace, classroom, home, and beyond. My hope is that this book provides a pathway to BREATHE as a part of your daily life.

Keywords: meditation, mindfulness, reflection, empathy, compassion, gratitude, understanding, cooperation, acceptance, well-being, breathe, stress reduction

> *To effectively communicate, we must realize*
> *that we are all different in the way we perceive*
> *the world and use this understanding as a*
> *guide to our communication with others.*
>
> —TONY ROBBINS

Contents

Introduction

Every breath we take, every step we make, can
be filled with peace, joy, and serenity.

—*Thich Nhat Hanh*

"Breath is the crux of human life. It is easy to take it for granted because most of us do it so automatically" (Swisa, 2013, p. 1). Remembering to breathe consciously became a pivotal moment in my work and spiritual practice. In this book, the word "breathe" is used both as a starting point and as an acronym, containing the following seven words: breathe, reflect, empathize, accept, thank, hearten, engage. Understand is included as well, because understanding is an essential component of a holistic approach to all learning, training and, most important, interpersonal relationships. These eight words have become the focus for my life work as an executive in the workplace and an educator in the classroom and beyond.

Each chapter includes at least one activity that is suitable for personal and/or professional use. All activities may be modified, depending on the needs of the individuals and the environment. The activities were originally written with a focus on the classroom and have been modified for the workplace, group activities, and personal practice. In any event, "classroom" may be used as a metaphor for learning wherever, whenever, and however that learning occurs. This chapter includes a brief activity that is beneficial when used on a daily basis to foster a sense of well-being and trust.

It was a conscious choice to use the verb form for each word rather than the noun form whenever possible. Verbs represent action. It is my hope that this book will encourage action on the part of the reader. However, understanding these concepts is the precursor to action. For this reason, both the noun forms, when discussing concepts, and the verb forms, when expressing action, are used throughout this book. Because these concepts are interconnected, certain topics may be discussed in more than one chapter.

The first chapter, "Breathe," provides the theme for this book. It discusses the use of breath as an introduction to mindfulness and meditation. To breathe and to pay attention to your breathing is the first step in the process toward greater mindfulness. Paying attention to your breath, without judgment, is the essence of mindfulness (Siegel, 2011, p. 83). This chapter discusses the benefits of meditation and provides a breath meditation recording that may be used privately, at home, in the workplace, in group activities, and in the classroom.

The second chapter, "Reflect," combines the guiding principles of the experiential learning cycle and the practice of self-reflection. These principles are important to learners as well as teachers. Greater awareness is an outgrowth of the reflective process (Barduhn, 1998, p. 63). Finding opportunities to integrate reflection into our daily practice enhances learning and personal development. The chapter concludes with activities to practice reflective processes.

"Empathize" begins by comparing the concepts of empathy and compassion. While a brief discussion of empathy is included, the chapter primarily focuses on self-compassion and compassion toward others. The connection between human suffering and compassion is explored. The language of compassion, based on Marshall Rosenberg's book, *Nonviolent Communication* (2003), is discussed in order to provide a framework and appropriate language for expressing our feelings, needs and requests. Two activities are included at the end of the chapter: a guided meditation, suitable for personal and professional use, and a follow-up activity practicing the use of nonviolent language.

Accepting ourselves and others with nonjudgment increases a sense of trust and security in the workplace and beyond. As discussed in "Breathe," nonjudgment is part of practicing mindfulness. This chapter combines elements from the preceding chapters, particularly mindfulness, nonjudgment, and compassion because acceptance and forgiveness are positive outgrowths when these concepts are put into action.

Finding new ways to thank and appreciate the unique experiences in our lives, our surroundings, and those with whom we interact, leads to a greater sense of personal contentment. It also strengthens the neuroplasticity in the brain (Borysenko, 2014). Teaching this to others is a skill that promotes community and cooperation. Expressing gratitude promotes personal health and well-being as well (Emmons, 2010). The chapter includes ideas for incorporating gratitude and appreciation into our lives on a daily basis.

Generally, to hearten is defined as to "make more cheerful." *Merriam-Webster* (http://www.merriam-webster.com/dictionary/hearten) includes "to give heart to" as another definition (http://www.merriam-webster.com/dictionary/hearten). Both of these definitions are incorporated into this chapter. Bringing more joy and laughter into our lives helps break down barriers. I know from personal experience, bringing more heart into the workplace and classroom creates a sense of safety, trust, cooperation, connection, and community for everyone. Suggested community builders and other activities are included.

"Engage," in this chapter, is used to mean participate or be involved. In my courses and workshops, my hope is always that learners participate and are involved. Participation and involvement are part of the learning process and contribute to a sense of cooperation and community. In a learning-centered environment, when participants engage fully, there is a synergy among the learners that builds over time, and strengthens the culture of collaboration. This allows participants to experience our interconnectedness with one another and provides an opening to expand this interconnectedness beyond ourselves and include all living beings and the natural world.

The chapter titled "Understand" integrates all of the previous chapters with an approach to intercultural and interpersonal understanding. When we are mindful and fully present for another person, and we listen to their words with acceptance, nonjudgment, and compassion, we begin to actively engage in the process of understanding. Charles A. Curran (1978) talks about "a changed inner-view, arrived at through understanding" (p. 53). Understanding results when the listener participates in the dialogue and asks discerning questions that facilitate the process for the seeker to find solutions for themselves (p. 55).

A stronger sense of community, collaboration, and connection is formed when we transform the concepts of breath, reflection, empathy, acceptance, thankfulness, heart (and joy), engagement (and participation), and understanding. It turns them into the actions to breathe, reflect, empathize, accept, thank, hearten, engage, and understand. When we include all of these concepts and actions in the workplace, classroom, home, and other daily activities, we provide opportunities that enrich the lives of everyone, promote a greater sense of community and cooperation, and hopefully lead us closer to a more peaceful world.

Daily Morning Activity

Creating a supportive environment in the workplace, classroom, and beyond—where people feel safe to express themselves freely—is an important part of life, and especially for the activities in this book. This activity may be used daily or as frequently as necessary. If time is extremely limited, consider focusing on steps 1 through 5.

Goal: to create a safe, trusting, supportive environment for oneself and the group.

1. Have participants stand in a circle.
2. Explain to participants that you want them to feel safe, supported, and comfortable, and that you are going to start with a brief warm-up activity to promote feelings of well-being.
3. Ask participants to take three deep breaths at their own pace.
4. Ask participants to raise their hands straight up over their heads while inhaling, and release their arms and stretch toward the ground while exhaling.
5. Repeat step 3, three times.
6. If time is very limited, skip to step 9.
7. If you have an additional five to ten minutes, have participants sit in a comfortable position, either in a chair or on the floor. Ask them to close their eyes, take a deep breath, and relax.
8. Lead them in a brief guided meditation, using the following script or a variation to your liking. I have included the meditation in dialogue form below, so that you may record your own version. I have also included a link to vocaroo.com (http://vocaroo.com/i/s1tmYUNP96jQ) if you prefer to listen to a prepared recording. (Vocaroo is a website that hosts audio recordings.)

Pause after each paragraph before continuing to allow participants to take a few deep breaths.

[Begin meditation]
Take a deep breath. Let your body relax. If at any point during this practice, you can't think of something, continuing taking deep breaths.

Think of one of your favorite places. Think about what it looks like, what it smells like, what it feels like, and what it sounds like. Take three deep breaths and enjoy the feeling of being in your favorite place.

Think of a time when you felt safe and secure. Feel that safety in your body. Take three deep breaths.

Now, think of something or someone that you are grateful for. It could be a person, place, or thing. Take three deep breaths.

Now think of something you are grateful for about yourself. Take three deep breaths.

Carry this feeling of gratitude, safety, relaxation, and well-being with you throughout your day. Take three deep breaths.

Open your eyes when you are ready.
[End meditation]

9. Have participants stand up and walk around the room, greet each person with a smile, and say a word, phrase, or sentence

that includes a greeting, an expression of kindness, or an expression of gratitude to each person.

10. Have everyone sit down.
11. Continue with the regular daily activities.

Chapter 1

Breathe

*While it may be simple to practice
mindfulness, it is not necessarily easy.*

—Jon Kabat-Zinn

We all know that the process of breathing, inhaling and exhaling, is necessary for all human life. Yet we don't spend very much time paying attention to our breath. This chapter uses breath to help focus on the present moment and pay attention while practicing mindfulness and meditation. As you read through this chapter, notice your breath as a first step in this process. This chapter also discusses the health benefits of meditation and includes a guided meditation that focuses on the breath. (Go ahead! Take a deep breath.)

Before we can focus on our breath, we need to understand a key obstacle to meditation: our thoughts and their connection to the human experience. Human life is made up of experiences. Each experience is a combination of actions, thoughts, emotional feelings, images, and physical sensations (Chopra, 2014). Our thoughts are the vehicles with which we find expression for our experiences. As a general rule, thoughts are about the past or the future (Chopra, 2004, p. 78). When considering a past experience, we reflect on what we did, what we felt (sensations), how we felt (feelings), what we saw, and what we thought about the experience. Similarly, when thinking about the future, we think about what we will do, what we will feel (sensations), how we will feel (feelings), what we will see, and what we will think about the experience. We rarely spend time focusing our attention on the present moment.

This attention focused on the present moment is the essence of meditation. Meditation is the process of focusing "your attention while... witnessing the thought forms that come and go in your mind" (Chopra, 2004, p. 78) with detachment and nonjudgment. Finding an aid for focused attention helps the process of meditation. The breath is readily accessible, and therefore a good tool to use in meditation.

Chopra's use of the term "thought forms" provides a path toward detachment and nonjudgment about our thoughts. If we consider thoughts as forms instead of intrinsic to our personal identity, then we can begin to detach from thoughts as they arise during meditation. Developing nonjudgment and detachment when thoughts arise during meditation takes practice. By using breath as a focal point rather than thoughts, we begin the process of detachment.

Meditation has many health benefits. It reduces stress, thereby reducing stress hormones, like cortisol and adrenaline. The reduction of stress results in a strengthened immune system. Meditation helps your brain focus, learn, and grow.

A study led by Harvard University and Massachusetts General Hospital found that after only eight weeks of meditation, participants experienced beneficial growth in the brain areas associated with memory, learning, empathy, self-awareness, and stress regulation (the insula, hippocampus, and prefrontal cortex). In addition, the meditators reported decreased feelings of anxiety and greater feelings of calm. This study adds to the expanding body of research about the brain's amazing plasticity and ability to change habitual stress patterns (McGreevey, 2011).

In addition, meditation increases the flow of oxygen in the body. Meditation decreases depression, anxiety, and insomnia by releasing serotonin and endorphins (https://chopra.com/ccl/why-meditate-0). As a result, meditation also promotes a more positive attitude. This, in turn, benefits interpersonal relationships. It also contributes to greater productivity in one's professional life and personal life (Seppälä, 2013).

The words meditation and mindfulness are often used interchangeably. Meditation may take many forms; there are walking meditations, sitting meditations, and so on. An important outcome of meditation is improved mindfulness. Mindfulness means paying attention to our experiences, including our thoughts, sensations, feelings, and images while they are happening, without judgment and with acceptance (Kabat-Zinn, 1994, p. 4). Meditation practice is often a precursor to mindfulness because mindfulness becomes the way we demonstrate the practice of meditation in our daily lives.

One final thought to keep in mind: meditation is often referred to as a practice. Some may think of the word "practice" in terms of preparing for a performance or presentation. Educators often use the term to pertain to beliefs or methodologies. This is probably closer to the meaning of practice as it applies to meditation. Just as our professional practices improve and change with time, so does our meditation practice. The more we do it, the more refined our practice becomes.

Breathe Activity

Breath Meditation

This meditation may be used in the workplace, classroom, small groups, or privately. It is based on the stabilizing attention meditation from the foundation course for cognitively based compassion training (Negi, 2015). I have included the meditation in dialogue form below, so that you may record your own version. I have also included a link (http://vocaroo.com/i/s0ZzB2cLT28O) if you prefer to listen to a prepared recording. The dialogue is meant as a starting point. If any of the language feels awkward or uncomfortable, the facilitator or meditator may change any of the language as desired.

This is a helpful introduction for new meditators, accessible to all English language levels. The language is intentionally easy to understand. I have used this meditation, and participants have responded favorably. This meditation may be used in a variety of situations—home, workplace, or classroom. It relaxes and calms participants. It is a nice way to conclude an activity (prior to a final reflection) so that participants carry that sense of calm with them throughout the remainder of the day.

Goal: to experience mindfulness and learn a simple meditation that may be used regularly.

This meditation is composed of three parts. The introduction includes new vocabulary and an introductory discussion of the topic. The second part is the actual meditation portion. This may require listening to the meditation more than once and focusing on different elements each time. The post phase provides the opportunity to reflect on the activity, including the exploration of next steps.

Introduction:

1. Introduce the concept of meditation. Find out who has meditated and who meditates regularly. Find out what they know about meditation. Find out if anyone is uncomfortable with the idea of meditation. (The idea of meditation as a religion might come up. If it does, explain the scientific benefits of meditation discussed in this chapter.)
2. Introduce any new vocabulary, e.g., diaphragm, nonjudgment, mindfulness, third eye. Before beginning the meditation, ask the participants to notice how they are feeling physically and mentally. Ask them to share with a partner or with the group.

Meditation:

In this phase, the facilitator may or may not find it helpful to play relaxing music in the background. Some people find music distracting; others find it a helpful way to tune out external noises. You may read or play the following:

[Begin Meditation]

This is a meditation that focuses on the breath.

Find a comfortable position. You may sit in a chair or on the floor. If you sit in a chair, try to keep your feet flat on the floor or in a cross-legged position. If you sit on the floor, you may sit on a pillow for comfort and try to sit in a comfortable cross-legged position. Keep your back straight and shoulders broad. Place your hands in your lap or on your thighs, palms facing up in a relaxed position.

Gently close your eyes. Your gaze may be toward the floor or toward your third eye. (Your third eye is located about one inch above and between your eyes.) Notice any tension you may feel in your body. Try to relax any areas of tension that you notice.

Now begin to notice your breath. As you breathe, try to release any negative thoughts, feelings, or criticism. When you inhale, notice how the breath feels entering through the nostrils, and then feel your diaphragm as it expands. Now exhale and release the breath. Notice how it feels when your diaphragm contracts and the air exits through your nostrils. Repeat this three times.

You may notice, as you try to pay attention to your breath, that thoughts enter into your mind during this meditation. You may worry that you are doing something wrong. This is natural. Thoughts will come and go. Allow them to come and go without blame or criticism or judgment. Simply observe that you had a thought, and let it go. Allow yourself to return your focus to your breath.

If you find it challenging to focus on the flow of your breath, count evenly while you inhale and while you exhale, using the same count for both the inhale and exhale. This may be helpful.

Continue to focus on your breath. Continue to stay in the present moment with your breath.

Simply notice when thoughts arise, with acceptance and without criticism and judgment, and return to the focus on your breath. Enjoy this opportunity to place your attention in the present moment by focusing on your breath.

Continue to focus on your breath. Gently allow thoughts to enter and leave without judgment or criticism.

We will now conclude this breath meditation. As you continue with your day, if possible, remember a moment of peace or nonjudgment that you experienced during this meditation. We will conclude this meditation by sending peace, happiness, harmony, and healing to ourselves, our friends and loved ones, and all living beings.
[End Meditation]

Post Phase:

The post phase is the opportunity for reflection. Discussion may include any combination of writing, reading, speaking, and listening individually, in pairs, small groups, or with the whole group.

1. Here are some possible questions:
    a. Was this difficult? Easy? Why?
    b. Did you feel comfortable? Why or why not?
    c. What happened when you had thoughts?
    d. Do you feel different after meditating? Why or why not?

    e. What are the differences that you notice?

    f. Would you like to do this again? If participants would like to do this again, consider making it part of the routine.

2. As part of the post discussion, it might be helpful to review the benefits of meditation to their health and well-being. Review the health benefit discussion on pages 2-3 in this chapter.

Chapter 2

Reflect

Reflection requires space and time...
Stillness and quieting the mind foster deep reflection.

—BAUBACK YEGANEH

Reflection has been discussed and explored in academic circles for decades. This chapter begins by exploring the meaning of reflection from two pedagogic perspectives. Dewey's (1910) explanation of reflection represents the more traditional pedagogic approach, whereas Schön's (1983) discussion of reflection-in-action provides a pathway to the Eastern concept of reflection and mindfulness (Tremmel, 1993, p. 443). The concept of awareness as it relates to mindfulness and reflection leads to an exploration of the experiential learning cycle that differs from Kolb (Kolb, 1984, p. 41). This chapter concludes with an activity that includes aspects of mindfulness and reflection.

When discussing reflection in pedagogical circles, there is often an emphasis on analysis and problem solving (Clift, 1990, p. 211). Dewey

(2012) defines reflective thought as a "conscious and voluntary effort to establish belief based on a firm basis of reasons" (p. 5). Dewey continues by saying that doubt must be present as part of the reflective process (p. 8). He outlines the five steps of reflection as

1. identifying a difficulty;
2. defining the difficulty;
3. explaining the difficulty or exploring a possible solution;
4. using reasoning to explore more thoroughly; and
5. forming a conclusion (pp. 66–70).

This description of the reflective process is challenging for me because I don't believe that the presence of a difficulty is necessary for reflection to occur. For me, the focus of the reflective process is observation of a past experience. Reflective observation may occur either in the presence or absence of conflict.

In contrast to Dewey, Schön's reflection-in-action is a starting point to move from the more rational and analytical understanding of reflection posited by Dewey to a concept of reflection that aligns more closely with mindfulness (Tremmel, 1993, p. 442). As does mindfulness, reflection-in-action focuses on paying attention to what is happening in the present moment. Schön (1983) uses the term "think on your feet" to describe this (p. 53). Thinking on your feet is a metaphor for thinking while doing.

Mindfulness and reflection have similarities and differences. Both involve paying attention. As mentioned in the previous chapter, mindfulness means paying attention to our experiences, including our thoughts, sensations, feelings, and images, while they are happening—in the *present* moment, without judgment and with acceptance (Kabat-Zinn, 1994, p. 4). For me, reflection is the observation and description of thoughts, feelings, sensations, and images as they relate to an experience that occurred in the past. While reflection generally happens after an experience, greater mindfulness during an experience deepens the reflective process. Awareness is the third part of the process. Awareness is the result of the insight and knowledge gained from reflecting on an experience.

Mindfulness involves doing; one is paying attention in the present moment while participating in the act of doing something. Reflection involves seeing or observing; one is observing and describing what happened during the prior action. As a consequence of the insight and knowledge gained from doing and seeing, a new sense of being develops and evolves. This being or awareness is then integrated into future experiences.

In the figure below, I have modified David Kolb's experiential learning cycle (ELC) to reflect the connection between mindfulness (doing), reflection (seeing), and awareness (being) from Kolb's description of the ELC: experiencing, reflection, thinking, and acting (Yeganeh, 2009, p. 10). Kolb's experiential learning theory has transformed the paradigm for learning by defining learning as "the process whereby knowledge is created through the transformation of experience" (Kolb, 1984, p. 41).

The following figure creates a three-pronged version of the experiential learning cycle: doing (mindfulness) is closely aligned with Kolb's experiencing; seeing (reflection) is similar to Kolb's explanation of reflection, which is based on observation; and being, which is Kolb's thinking and acting combined in a singular concept (awareness). Kolb has referred to the ELC as a cycle or spiral because there is an element of advancement and transformation in the process (Yeganeh, 2009, p. 15). Both cycle and spiral images are important in the do-see-be version as well because progression and advancement are integral to learning. As our mindful attention improves, our intellectual muscle that allows us to reflect and observe improves. In turn, we gain more awareness.

Greater awareness results in greater mindfulness, which results in greater reflection, and so on. The more we learn, the more we grow.

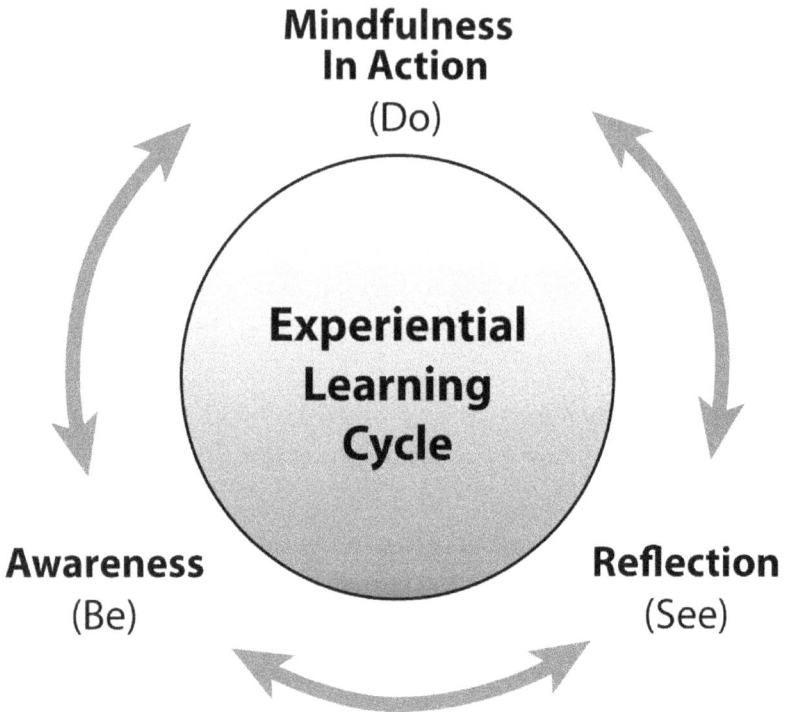

**Mindfulness
In Action
(Do)**

**Experiential
Learning
Cycle**

**Awareness
(Be)**

**Reflection
(See)**

Figure 1. Experiential Learning Cycle by Maxine Swisa

In order to create meaningful reflection for ourselves and others, it is important for us to reflect in stillness. Stillness implies the absence of distractions. The absence of distractions affords the possibility for heightened focus during the reflective process. Lao Tzu said, "One cannot reflect in streaming water. Only those who know internal peace can give it to others" (Lao Tzu, 604–531 BC). This quote describes the importance of stillness. It also offers two additional insights. First, it includes an aspect of reflection that has not yet been explicitly stated: reflection as an act of seeing ourselves. While this is not always necessary as part of the reflective process, personal reflection provides opportunities for personal growth as well as intellectual growth. Second, Lao Tzu, in the *Tao Te Ching* often used references to nature. Nature is a great starting point for a reflection activity. It is included in the activity on the following page.

This chapter has explored the interconnectedness of mindfulness, reflection, and awareness. Dewey, Schön, and Kolb have provided crucial perspectives on the reflective and learning processes. Dewey's focus is on the analytical reflective process. Schön's emphasis is on mindful reflection-in-action. Kolb discusses the importance of experience, observation, thinking, and acting. Reflection may be externally oriented, as is the case in the nature activity (pp. 14–15), or it may be internally oriented, as in the self-reflection activity (pp. 16–17). The important thing is to experience mindfully, observe reflectively, and continue to expand personal awareness.

Reflect Activities

This reflection activity has three parts and may be divided into three separate activities. The combined reflection activities accommodate multiple learning styles. This activity may be modified depending on the individual needs of the participants and the learning environment.

Mindfulness (Do):

Goal: to practice paying attention in the present moment.

This activity begins with a walk outdoors in nature. This is helpful for kinesthetic, visual, and tactile learning. This is the mindful *do* portion of the activity trilogy.

1. Before beginning, review the concept of mindfulness with the participants, emphasizing the importance of paying attention to everything they experience in the present moment.
2. Hopefully, at the very least, there is a tree or a bush outside the building. If there is, take your participants outside and have them select one article of nature. If there isn't access to nature nearby, bring in some leaves, twigs, flowers, or other natural finds to share with the group.
3. Once the participants have an object, remind them to pay attention to as many details as they can about that object. Encourage them to use as many of the five senses as possible. (Taste may not be advisable, depending on the object!) This activity may be done in pairs or small groups.

4. Once the participants have spent enough time (three to five minutes) focusing on the objects, have the groups share with one another everything they experienced.

While the primary focus is on "doing," this activity also includes reflection, similar to Schön's description of reflection-in-action because an important part of paying attention in this activity includes observation. Part of the observation process is the ability to express these observations either orally or in writing.

Reflection (See):

Goal: to develop greater ability to observe.

This activity begins with a community builder and continues with a self-reflection activity.

1. Community builder: the mirror game
   a. Participants stand in two lines facing each other.
   b. Each person in one line has a partner in the other line.
   c. Both lines take turns leading the activity and following the activity.
   d. The leaders initiate movement or facial expression.
   e. The followers act as a mirror for the leaders.
   f. When the facilitator says, "Freeze," both lines freeze and observe themselves and their partners carefully.
   g. They take a moment to share what they observe.

This community builder is meant to be playful. It is a safe way to prepare for the second part of this activity that focuses on personal reflection.

2. Self-Reflection. Colored pencils or markers are needed.
   a. The personal reflection begins by observing one's reflection in a small mirror.
   b. Participants have one minute to *observe* as many things about themselves as possible. Encourage them to pay attention to any thoughts, feelings, images, and actions that they notice. Encourage them to be mindful.
   c. The participants then sit down and begin a process known as freewriting (Tremmel, 1993, p. 449). Freewriting involves writing down everything that comes to mind, with no filter. If participants seem confused, discuss the concept of stream of consciousness. Encourage them to use that concept when writing. Tell the participants that this is for their eyes only; they will not share this. Give them as much time as they need to complete this. It is important that they work in stillness and quiet.

      This activity can be challenging for many reasons. Participants don't know what to write. They don't like what they write. They don't like what they see. Encourage them to explore these challenges as part of their reflective observation.
   d. When they are done, ask them to use another color pen or pencil, and to circle anything that they wrote that was judgmental.
   e. Ask them to notice how of much of the writing is covered in circles.
   f. Then, ask them to use a third color writing implement and see if they able to either rephrase the judgmental comments in a way that is more accepting or revise the judgment with a more accepting comment. For example, the description "messy hair" might be replaced with "uncombed hair."

g. Conclude this activity with a closing circle and have each participant share a nonjudgmental observation about themselves.

Awareness (Be):

Goal: to learn from the activities and gain greater self-awareness.

The third activity focuses on awareness. It is a synthesis of the insight and knowledge gained from the two previous activities.

1. Review the previous activities with the group.
2. Have participants share something that they learned about themselves or others. On the board, write, "What did I learn about myself? How might I apply this new awareness to challenges that might arise in the future?" Give participants time to think about these questions.
3. Have participants discuss their thoughts with a partner.
4. Have participants jot down the most important insight(s).
5. In closing, have participants share one insight with the group.

Chapter 3

Empathize

The essence of compassion is a desire to alleviate the suffering of others and to promote their well-being. This is the spiritual principle from which all other positive inner values emerge.

—His Holiness the Dalai Lama

This chapter primarily explores compassion. Empathy is discussed first, because there is often some confusion regarding the difference between empathy and compassion. The Cognitively-Based Compassion Training (2015) in Atlanta provided me with a great deal of insight into the relationship between empathy, compassion, suffering, and the human desire for happiness and well-being. The connection between these is discussed. In addition, both self-compassion and compassion toward others are examined. Marshall Rosenberg (2003) provides a process for expressing our feelings and needs as well as the language to do this. There are two activities included at the end of the chapter. The first is a self-compassion meditation activity. The second is a follow-up activity based on Marshall Rosenberg's work.

Empathy involves an emotional resonance with another person's experience (Dalai Lama, 2012, p. 55). Empathy is the ability to feel and understand another person's emotional state (http://www.merriam-webster.com/dictionary/empathy). "Seeing from another person's point of view: We sense the other's intentions and imagine what an event means in his or her mind" (Siegel, 2011, p. 28). Empathy allows us to "feel" what another person is feeling based on our ability to recall prior experiences that include similar emotions (Siegel, 2011, p. 28). These may be positive or negative feelings. We can empathically experience the joy a mother feels at the sight of her newborn baby, even if the mother is unknown to us. Likewise, we can empathically experience sorrow when we hear of the loss of another person's loved one.

While empathy pertains to either positive or negative emotional experiences, compassion is generally focused on difficulties that another person is experiencing. Compassion extends beyond feeling for another person's emotional state, and includes "a desire to *do* something to relieve the hardships of others" (Dalai Lama, 2012, p. 55). In his book, *Beyond Religion* (2012), His Holiness the Dalai Lama, attempts to transcend religious values to focus on a broader perspective: a secular view of human values that includes compassion as a basic *human* value (p. xiv). Nonetheless, it is clear that his beliefs stem from Buddhist beliefs, specifically the Four Noble Truths. Because there is no mention of God in the Four Noble Truths, it is easier to translate these concepts into secular terms than it might be with Judeo-Christian religious beliefs. The Four Noble Truths state

1. the truth of suffering; i.e., suffering exists;
2. the truth of the cause of suffering; i.e., there is a cause for suffering;

3. the truth of freedom from suffering; i.e., there is an end to suffering;
4. the truth of the way to eliminate suffering; i.e., there is a way to end suffering.

These four statements provide a guide to daily living that extends beyond Buddhist practice.

The first Noble Truth, the presence of suffering in life, has profound implications for all human interactions. When we acknowledge that all human beings experience some degree of suffering or discomfort, we begin to understand the meaning of compassion. As mentioned in the opening quote by His Holiness the Dalai Lama, compassion is the desire to relieve the suffering of others and to promote their well-being. When the desire to relieve suffering and promote well-being is directed inward, it is the beginning of self-compassion and is discussed on the following page.

The second Noble Truth discusses the cause of suffering, principally desire, our attachment to our desires, and the impermanence of all things in life (http://www.buddhanet.net/fundbud4.htm). Desire is a cause of suffering because it is impossible to satisfy all of our cravings. Desire originates in our thoughts. We think about something that we want, which in turn causes discomfort because we don't have it. A cycle of frustration, anger, or worry may follow; all these emotions perpetuate our distress.

The third Noble Truth says that there is an end to suffering (http://www.buddhanet.net/fundbud4.htm). The end is achieved through death or enlightenment. In secular terms, death is the end to suffering because as long as we are alive, we will experience some degree of suffering.

Having said that, the fourth Noble Truth states that the way to end suffering is through mindfulness and meditation (http://www.buddhanet.net/fundbud4.htm). If we experience greater mindfulness and meditate more, we have the possibility to experience less suffering. As we become more aware and less judgmental of our thoughts and our suffering, we begin to experience a greater sense of well-being. This in turn allows for a greater sense of compassion. In order to be truly compassionate of others, we must begin with self-compassion.

Self-compassion begins first by acknowledging any discomfort that we may feel. Often, we are not even aware of our discomfort. Meditation can help to raise our awareness because we tend to be more mindful of our thoughts and feelings during meditation. The next step is to notice our discomfort. As a general rule, this happens when thoughts and feelings arise regarding an unfulfilled desire for something (Negi, 2015). At this time, we have an opportunity to remind ourselves of our preference for happiness and well-being rather than discomfort. When we gain awareness of our desire to reduce discomfort, while practicing nonjudgment, we begin to understand the nature of self-compassion. By acknowledging that our ultimate goal is to seek fulfillment and happiness, we begin to remind ourselves to place our attention on this goal (Negi, 2015) and to avoid discomfort. In this way, we are able to practice self-compassion. Once we are able to practice self-compassion, it becomes easier to practice compassion toward others. We are able to do this when we realize that all human beings also want to reduce their suffering and increase their sense of well-being.

After understanding the nature of compassion, it is important to discuss the language of compassion as well. Marshall Rosenberg (2003) is one of the pioneers in this effort. In his book, *Nonviolent Communication* (NVC), he provides a framework for interacting with others and sharing observations, feelings, needs, and requests without blame or criticism, using nonjudgmental language (p. 6) with which individuals assume personal responsibility for these feelings, needs, and requests. These are explained as "[t]he concrete actions we *observe* that affect our well-being. How we *feel* in relation to what we observe. The *needs*, values, desires, etc. that create our feelings. The concrete actions we *request* in order to enrich our lives" (p. 7). The NVC process is about expressing honestly and receiving compassionately, using the four factors mentioned, i.e. observations, feelings, needs, and requests (p. 7). If we are able to express ourselves honestly and receive feedback without blame, criticism, or self-judgment, we may begin to experience greater well-being.

When discussing observations, Rosenberg (2003) mentions the importance of separating observation from evaluation (p. 30). Evaluation often involves an opinion or judgment. For example, there is a difference between these two statements: "Doug procrastinates" and "Doug only studies for exams the night before" (p. 30). The first is an evaluation because the language used implies a criticism of Doug's approach to studying. The second is an observation because there is no value judgment, just the observation describing when Doug studies for exams.

Rosenberg continues by discussing vocabulary to express genuine feelings for when our needs are being met and when they are not being met. Examples of words that express feelings when our needs are being met include "appreciative, calm, comfortable, delighted, encouraged, fulfilled, happy" (p. 44). Examples of words that express feelings when our needs are not being met include "afraid, angry, disappointed, discouraged, hesitant, troubled, uncomfortable" (pp. 46–47). When we use nonviolent language to honestly express our feelings, it is important to remember that there are no right or wrong feelings. Practicing mindfulness helps this process because it allows us to remove the elements of judgment or criticism. When we are mindful of our feelings, we allow ourselves the freedom to express them with clarity.

The next factor that Rosenberg discusses is the necessity to express our needs without blaming or criticizing ourselves or others (p. 50). As discussed earlier, all human beings share the basic need for well-being. Some words that may be used to express these needs include "creativity, acceptance, appreciation, love, respect, trust, warmth, peace" (pp.

54–55). It is important to express our needs without blaming or criticizing others for not meeting them. An example of the former is "It's so annoying that you're always late." The first obstacle in the statement is the use of the word "always." This immediately implies criticism and puts the person on the defensive. A statement that would exemplify Rosenberg's process is "I feel frustrated when you come late to pick me up because I need to get to work on time." In this statement, the speaker takes responsibility for his/her own feelings. It includes the observation that the listener arrived late without blaming that person. It concludes by expressing what the speaker needs. Once again, mindfulness facilitates the process because we are better equipped to express our needs with clarity and nonjudgment.

The final step in the NVC process is to request what we want using "clear, positive, concrete, language" (p. 70). It is also important to request what we want without making the other person feel defensive or inadequate. A statement such as "I need you to understand me" is unclear. However, if we say, "Please let me know what you heard me say," it allows the listener to respond to a specific request (p. 88). This provides an atmosphere for discussion that may lead to greater understanding.

Combining Rosenberg's language of compassion with the practice of compassion in human relationships is the pathway to greater well-being for ourselves and others. When we begin to practice self-compassion by paying attention to our thoughts, feelings, and sensations, as well as the language we use to express them, we can then extend the practice of compassion toward others as we are able to realize that all human beings want to reduce their suffering and increase their sense of well-being. This broader perspective allows us to "widen our circle of compassion" (Einstein, 1950) to include more and more people, ultimately practicing this compassion toward everyone we meet.

Empathize Activities

I have included two activities for this chapter. The first is a group activity that focuses on self-compassion. The second is based on Marshall Rosenberg's book, *Nonviolent Communication* (2003).

Activity 1: Self-Compassion Meditation

The self-compassion activity is suitable may be modified to meet the needs of your group. This meditation activity is divided into three phases. The introduction includes new vocabulary and discussion of the topic. The meditation phase includes the actual listening portion. The post phase is the opportunity to reflect on the activity, including the exploration of next steps. This meditation is also based on the Cognitively-Based Compassion Training (CBCT).

Goal: to practice meditation and experience compassion through meditation.

Introduction:

1. Begin by writing the word "compassion" on the board. Ask participants what the word means. If the word "empathy" is mentioned, discuss the differences.
2. Review the definitions of mindfulness and meditation. Make sure to include the concepts of paying attention and experiencing acceptance and nonjudgment. If applicable, ask participants what they remember about the previous meditation activity, particularly posture and breath.

3. Discuss any other vocabulary that may be needed such as aspiration, expectation, inadequacy, perspective.
4. Tell them that this is a meditation on self-compassion.

Meditation Phase:

If you decide to read this meditation yourself, it may be nice to play soothing, meditation music while reading. I have included a recording of the meditation as well (http://vocaroo.com/i/s0aJFAMKpxo8).

[Begin meditation]
This meditation focuses on self-compassion. We will pay attention to some of the causes of our personal discomfort, we will work to relieve them, and we will work to create a deeper sense of well-being.

Find a comfortable position either sitting in a chair or on the floor. Keep your back straight and shoulders broad. Place your hands in your lap or on your thighs, palms facing up in a relaxed position. Gently close your eyes. Notice if you are feeling any tension in your body. Take three slow deep breaths. As you exhale, release any tension you may be feeling in your body.

Take a moment to remember a time when you felt nurtured and safe. As you think about this, try to embody these qualities so that you can continue to feel that same sense of nurturing and safety. Take a deep breath while you experience these feelings. Breathe in. Breathe out. Relax.

Continue feeling a sense of safety while focusing on your breathing. Practice being present while you're breathing, and pay attention to the inhalation and exhalation of your breath. Breathe in. Breathe out. Relax. Notice any thoughts, feelings, and sensations that you may be experiencing. Allow these thoughts, feelings, and sensations to come and go without blame or criticism or judgment. Simply observe that you had a thought or feeling or sensation, and let it go. Allow yourself to return your focus to your breath. Breathe in. Breathe out. Relax.

Now take a moment to think about your desire for happiness and well-being, and also think about your desire to avoid disappointment and unhappiness. Think about how your desire for happiness is the basis for all of your thoughts, hopes, and expectations.

Take a moment to reflect on your current experiences and think about the aspects that are challenging to you; think about the things that threaten your happiness and contribute to the suffering that you want to avoid. You might experience this as fear, loss, criticism, blame, or lack of recognition. You may feel frustration or worry about not getting things you want, such as material or professional success, praise, or respect. You may also feel badly about your inadequacies or imperfections.

After you identify some of the reasons for these challenges, take a few moments to reflect on them while also thinking about the bigger picture. Try to remember that events, losses, failures, illnesses, and other limitations happen not only to you, but to every human being.

Reflect on the fact that these situations are the result of many causes and conditions over which none of us has full control. Pay attention and see if this shift in attitude allows for accepting these imperfections and difficulties with a greater sense of kindness toward yourself and less judgment and blame.

How much of your unhappiness results from being too focused on desires for material gain, social and professional status, and praise and recognition from others? Think about how none of these can be truly lasting or permanent. Once you are able to accept that nothing is lasting or permanent in our lives, take a few moments to think about this more deeply.

Take a few deep breaths, and treat yourself with kindness, love, and compassion when thinking of the struggles and challenges that arise in your life. Once again, remember that all human beings experience struggles and challenges, and that all of these thoughts, feelings, sensations, and experiences are impermanent. Breathe in. Breathe out. Relax.

During this meditation, you may notice you feel a greater sense of ease as you accept the reality of our lives and the challenges of all human beings. Note how shifting this perspective can lead to greater relief, comfort, and inner peace. Breathe in. Breathe out. Relax.

Set your intention to release yourself from suffering, and focus on your deep desire for well-being and happiness.

Let's conclude this meditation by sending thoughts of well-being, compassion, love, and happiness to every living being on the earth.

Post Phase:

The post phase is the opportunity for reflection. Discussion may include any combination of writing, reading, speaking, and listening individually, in pairs, small groups, or with the whole group.

1. This is an opportunity for participants to reflect on this meditation. If you have done the breath meditation with the group, ask them a few questions about the two experiences. Here are some suggestions.
   a. Was this the same as the breath meditation? Why or why not?
   b. What did you like about this meditation?
   c. What was challenging?
   d. Did you experience any thoughts of discomfort?
   e. What happened when you had thoughts?
   f. Do you feel different after meditating? Why or why not?
   g. Do you feel more compassionate toward yourself? Toward others? Why or why not?
2. If you are not in a circle, ask participants to stand or sit in a circle. Go around the circle and ask them to share one thing they learned.
3. Conclude this activity with a one-word reflection. Ask each participant to say one word (or sentence) about how he or she feels.

Activity 2: The Language of Compassion

This activity is based on Marshall Rosenberg's book, *Nonviolent Communication* (2003). It is important for the facilitator to have access to this book in order to conduct this activity. The book provides a process for nonviolent communication. This activity explores this process in more depth.

Goal: to develop greater awareness of the importance of the words we use when communicating feelings, needs, and requests.

1. Introduce the concepts of nonviolent communication as discussed in Rosenberg's book, *Nonviolent Communication*, and on pages 22–24 in this book.
2. Review language and vocabulary that promotes compassionate communication. Some of this information is listed on pages 209–210 in Rosenberg's book and included in the appendix.
3. Have participants work in pairs. Give them a moment to think of a person with whom they have experienced some difficulty or conflict.
4. Have each participant describe the situation to his or her partner.
5. Have the pairs role-play each situation two times.
   a. The first time will be using language that they might have actually used in the situation or might have used in the past.
   b. The second time will be using the words and language that Rosenberg suggests. Participants will practice expressing their observations, feelings, needs, and requests and listen to their partner's observations, feelings, needs, and requests without blame or criticism.
6. Have participants reflect on the role-playing activities with their partner. What differences did they notice between the two instances? Was it challenging to use or think of the appropriate nonviolent language?
7. To wrap up, participants will come together as a group and reflect on the experience. Some possible questions include
   a. What were some of the challenges you found when using compassionate language?
   b. Which specific language would you use?

c. Would you like to incorporate this language into your daily activities?
d. Do you have any other thoughts or ideas?
e. In conclusion, would you share one thing you learned from this activity?

Chapter 4

Accept

Grant me the serenity to accept the things I cannot change.

—*RUDOLPH NIEBUHR*

While researching for this chapter, I came upon the Serenity Prayer by Rudolph Niebuhr (1892–1971). Accepting our challenges with serenity (Niebuhr, 1951) is not easy. To accept requires the practice of mindfulness, nonjudgment, the absence of blame and criticism, and the ability to forgive ourselves and other people. In addition, the language for nonviolent communication is an important skill for expressing acceptance, nonjudgment, and forgiveness. Nonjudgment precedes acceptance, and acceptance precedes forgiveness. When we are able to integrate all of this into our daily thoughts, feelings, sensations, and actions, we are able to experience life with greater serenity and inner peace. An activity is included to augment the personal exploration of nonjudgment, acceptance, and forgiveness.

The first step toward acceptance is nonjudgment. Before we can truly embrace the practice of nonjudgment, we need to understand the nature of judgment. All human beings spend a great deal of time evaluating whether something is good or bad. This is the essence of judgment (Kabat-Zinn, 1994, p. 55). Rosenberg (2003) expands on the concept of judgment by discussing moralistic judgments and value judgments (pp. 15–17). "Moralistic judgments imply wrongness or badness on the part of people who don't act in harmony with our values" (p. 15). 'Value judgments' are the qualities we value in life; for example, we might value honesty, freedom, or peace…We make *moralistic* judgments of people who fail to support our value judgments; for example 'Violence is bad. People who kill others are evil.' Had we been raised speaking a language that facilitated the expression of compassion, we would have learned to articulate our needs and values directly, rather than to insinuate wrongness when they have not been met. For example, instead of 'Violence is bad,' we might say. 'I am fearful of the use of violence to resolve conflicts; I value the resolution of human conflicts through other means'" (p. 17).

When we think and speak in morally judgmental terms, we create barriers between ourselves and other people.

Behaviors and language that often go hand in hand with judgment are blame and criticism. Blame involves placing the responsibility on someone when something bad happens (http://www.merriam-webster.com/dictionary/blame). This often includes using judgmental language. When we hear this type of negative language, we may internalize that judgment and blame ourselves. Conversely, we may blame the other person for being rude, selfish, inconsiderate, and so on (Rosenberg, 2003, pp. 49–50). We may even blame ourselves *and* the other person. Blame is a way to escape responsibility for our thoughts, feelings, or actions by saying things like, "I messed up. I can't do anything right" (Kabat-Zinn, 1994, p. 196). If the blame is placed on the other person, the statement would be "You messed up. You can't do anything right." Whereas blame places the responsibility for an action on someone, criticism expresses disapproval (http://www.merriam-webster.com/dictionary/criticism) of a person's actions or character traits. An example of criticism might be "You're irresponsible," or "I'm irresponsible." Both blame and criticism involve negative forms of language and judgments, and both create barriers among the participants when communicating, even if the negativity is self-directed.

Now that the concepts of judgment, blame, and criticism have been discussed, it is time to focus on the use of nonjudgmental language as part of daily communication, especially when expressing thoughts, feelings, needs, and requests. Being mindful of our thoughts and feelings is a first step in this process. As mentioned in chapter 1, mindfulness is paying attention to our experiences, including our thoughts, sensations, feelings, and images while they are happening, without judgment and with acceptance (Kabat-Zinn, 1994, p. 4). It is important to note that judging things is part of being human (p. 56). However, it is also important to remember to notice it without getting emotionally involved in that judgment. "A nonjudging orientation…means that we can act with greater clarity in our own lives, and be more balanced, more effective, and more ethical in our activities" (p. 57). When we become more mindful, we gain clarity regarding our thoughts, feelings, and needs. As we gain clarity, we are able to incorporate this into our interactions with ourselves and other people by using nonjudgmental language that is free of blame and criticism. When we use language that expresses our personal feelings and needs while not condemning others for their feelings and needs, we begin an important step toward communicating in a nonjudgmental manner. This paves the way for compassionate communication and greater understanding.

Marshall Rosenberg (2003) provides some examples of nonjudgmental language, free of blame and criticism. For example, expressing our feelings and needs to a friend who cancels plans might include language like: "I felt disappointed when you didn't come over, because I wanted to talk over some things that were bothering me" (p. 50). Speakers take ownership for their feelings and explain why they feel as they do. A helpful template to use, based on Rosenberg's example, when expressing feelings and needs is: I feel _____ because I needed (or wanted)_____. We are not judging ourselves or the other person, but we are clearly describing our feelings and needs. By taking responsibility for our own feelings and needs, we remove the burden of blame from the recipient. This type of nonjudgmental language allows both parties to communicate openly and honestly.

Once we are mindful of our thoughts, feelings, sensations, and needs and are able to express them nonjudgmentally, we are then ready to explore the process of accepting ourselves and other people. When we mindfully pay attention in the present moment without judgment (Kabat-Zinn, 1994, p. 4), we are setting the stage for acceptance to occur. The essence of acceptance is going with the flow. This means letting go of preconceived ideas or expectations of what "should" happen and accepting what is actually happening as it unfolds (p. 53). "Letting go is only possible if we can bring awareness and acceptance to the nitty-gritty of just how stuck we can get" (p. 54). Acceptance and awareness allow us to acknowledge our challenges as part of our existence without resisting them. We are able to pay attention in the present moment and notice that we are experiencing, without judgment, a difficult situation.

Accept—then act. Whatever the present moment contains, accept it as if you had chosen it. Always work with it, not against it. Make it your friend and ally, not your enemy. This will miraculously transform your whole life (Tolle, 1999, p. 29).

When we accept whatever comes our way as if we had "chosen it," we are empowering ourselves to make peace with challenges or difficulties that arise. This is the idea behind the serenity of acceptance. We accept that all is as it is meant to be at this moment.

Once we are able to accept life experiences as they occur and go with the flow of life, we are ready to forgive. Acceptance plants the seeds from which the flower of forgiveness blooms. Letting go is an important part of forgiveness, just as it is for acceptance. Letting go allows us to release old feelings and experiences of negativity. "Forgiveness is…a movement to let go of the pain, the resentment, the outrage that you have carried as a burden for so long" (Kornfield, 1993, p. 284). We don't have to condone the action in order to forgive. We forgive in order to release ourselves from the burden of carrying negative feelings toward ourselves or other people. True forgiveness can free us from holding on to bad feelings that weigh us down (Swisa, 2013, p. 49). In this way, forgiveness is an act of liberation; it lightens our emotional load. Forgiveness is one of the greatest kindnesses we can bestow upon ourselves (p. 50). When we accept that all of us have made mistakes, and consequently let go of our internal sources of disapproval and judgment, we are able to truly forgive, and release ourselves from the emotional weight that carrying anger, frustration, and other negativity entails.

When we are able to transform judgment, blame, and criticism into nonjudgment, acceptance, and forgiveness, we are able to live with greater inner peace. Mindfulness is an important part of this process and allows us to practice nonjudgment. Going with the flow allows us to accept the present moment as it happens. Releasing stored feelings of negativity allows us to experience the joyful gift of forgiveness. As we remember to pay attention and practice mindfulness, we are able to find the language of compassion, which in turn leads to nonjudgment, acceptance, and forgiveness for ourselves and other people and ultimately greater peace, serenity, and well-being for all.

Accept Activities

I have included two activities for this chapter. The first is an activity that focuses on nonjudgment and acceptance. The second focuses on forgiveness.

Activity 1: Nonjudgment and Acceptance

This activity is taken from Deepak Chopra's book *The Seven Spiritual Laws of Success* (1994). These are suggested activities and may be modified according to the needs of the participants. This is best done at the beginning of an activity, so that participants can practice paying attention to their language usage and thoughts during the activity, and possibly extend the exercise for longer than one session.

Goal: to practice mindfulness, nonjudgment, and acceptance.

Introduction

1. Discuss vocabulary: judgment, blame, criticism, nonjudgment, acceptance, go with the flow, let go
2. Pair practice or small groups: Ask participants to discuss a recent experience that involved any of the vocabulary listed above.

Acceptance Activity

1. Write on the board: "Today, I will practice acceptance. I will accept people, situations, circumstances, and events as they occur.

I accept things as they are at this moment... I will remind myself of this throughout the day" (Chopra, 1994, p. 63).

2. Ask participants to write this in their journal (preferably) or notebook.

3. *Pair practice.* Ask participants to discuss what they understand this to mean.

4. *Group activity.* Share some ideas with the entire group to make sure the participants understand this message.

5. *Pair practice.* Ask one participant to talk about an experience in the past day that was difficult to accept. Have the other participant listen for judgmental language, blame or criticism. Discuss any observations. Switch.

6. *Group activity.* Discuss any observations, including use of language, thoughts, and feelings with the whole group.

7. Ask participants to carry around the quote from point number one until the next meeting. Remind them to be mindful and pay attention to at least one time that they have difficulty accepting a given situation or person and were able to turn the situation around, accept it, and go with the flow.

8. Ask participants to describe the experience and write about it in their journals.

9. Remind them to bring the journals to the next session. Follow up and discuss the experiences in the next session.

Closing Activity

In the closing circle, have participants reflect on this activity. Was it easy? Difficult? Do they find it easy to accept situations as they arise? Why or why not? What is one thing they learned?

Activity 2: Forgiveness Confetti

These are suggested activities and may be modified according to the needs of your participants.

Goal: to practice and experience forgiveness.

Introduction

1. Discuss vocabulary: forgiveness, resentment, acceptance, let go
2. *Small group discussion.* Why is forgiveness important?
3. *Group discussion.* Share some insights with the group.

Forgiveness Activity

1. Put on some relaxing background music.
2. Erase anything that might be on the board and write one word: "forgiveness."
3. Hand out colorful strips of paper.
4. Tell participants that what they write during this activity is for their eyes only. Tell them to use one strip of paper for each instance. Ask them to briefly describe a person or situation that they would like to forgive, including themselves.
5. When participants are done writing, have them read their strips of paper to themselves, and think about how it feels to forgive themselves, a particular person, or a situation.
6. When they are ready, have them tear up each strip into tiny pieces.
7. Once all participants are done, play festive, positive music, like "Let It Go" by Idina Menzel (https://www.youtube.com/

watch?v=moSFlvxnbgk) or "Best Day of My Life" by American Authors (https://www.youtube.com/watch?v=Y66j_BUCBMY).

8. Have participants throw the tiny pieces of paper into the air like confetti and focus on forgiveness while dancing, singing, and moving to the music.

Closing Activity

In the closing circle, have participants reflect on this activity. Was it easy to forgive? Difficult? What is one word to describe how you're feeling right now?

Chapter 5

Thank

It's not happiness that makes us grateful,
it's gratefulness that makes us happy.

—*David Steindl-Rast*

To thank others and express gratitude to others are important steps that lead to a happier existence. Gratitude promotes greater health and well-being, which in turn leads to greater happiness. This chapter will explore the benefits of gratitude for our physical health, emotional well-being, and interpersonal relationships based on research by Robert Emmons, PhD, professor of psychology at University of California–Davis. Because of the neuroplasticity of our brain, even when we don't naturally feel grateful, we are able to rewire our brain by exercising the gratitude muscle and training ourselves to experience more gratitude in our lives (Siegel, 2011, p. 39). Some suggestions to help cultivate gratitude are included as well as a gratitude activity.

Emmons is one of the foremost authorities on the benefits of gratitude. He has been studying the effects of gratitude for over a decade. He has released findings about the benefits of gratitude (Emmons, 2010), particularly as it relates to physical health, psychological well-being, and interpersonal relationships.

Feeling grateful improves our physical health in several ways. Emmons remarked in a 2006 interview with Elizabeth Heubeck on www.webmd.com, "Grateful people take better care of themselves and engage in more protective health behaviors like regular exercise, a healthy diet, and regular physical examinations." Gratitude helps people manage stress better. When stress levels are lower, stress hormone levels are reduced. This, in turn, results in a strengthened immune system. Lower stress levels also contribute to lower blood pressure and better sleep patterns. Grateful people also tend to be more optimistic. Because of a more positive mental outlook, they have better results combatting health issues (Emmons, 2010). In addition, when facing adversity or trauma, "if people have a grateful disposition, they'll recover more quickly. I believe gratitude gives people a perspective from which they can interpret negative life events and help them guard against post-traumatic stress and lasting anxiety" (Emmons, 2010). If those health benefits aren't enough, positive emotions may add up to seven years to your life (Emmons, 2013)!

On a psychological level, gratefulness contributes to the ability to experience other positive emotions such as joy, happiness, and pleasure (Emmons, 2010). Grateful people experience fewer negative emotions like anger, jealousy, and envy (Emmons, 2010. As a result of experiencing less envy, for example, they have greater self-esteem because they aren't negatively comparing themselves with other people (Emmons, 2010). Gratitude increases feelings of happiness and decreases depression. Grateful people also tend to be more compassionate and less aggressive because they are able to appreciate the positive in situations (Emmons, 2010).

Some of the most significant benefits of practicing gratitude are social benefits. Emmons (2010) describes gratitude as having two parts:

> First, it's an affirmation of goodness. We affirm that there are good things in the world, gifts and benefits we've received. This doesn't mean that life is perfect; it doesn't ignore complaints, burdens, and hassles. But when we look at life as a whole, gratitude encourages us to identify some amount of goodness in our life... The second part of gratitude is figuring out where that goodness comes from. We recognize the sources of this goodness as being outside of ourselves. It didn't stem from anything we necessarily did ourselves...I think true gratitude involves a humble dependence on others: We acknowledge that other people—or even higher powers, if you're of a spiritual mind-set—gave us many gifts, big and small, to help us achieve the goodness in our lives.

Grateful people tend to be more forgiving and compassionate (Emmons, 2010). Grateful people feel a greater bond with other people. As a result, their interpersonal relationships tend to be more satisfying.

Amy Morin wrote an article for *Forbes* magazine (2014) discussing the social benefits of gratitude. She wrote that people are more likely to want to be friendly with you when you remember to thank them and express appreciation for something that they did. Remembering to acknowledge and thank people for little acts of kindness is a gift you give yourself and the other person. You feel better when you remember to thank someone, and they feel better because they feel recognized. These are some of the positive social benefits we reap when we express gratitude to ourselves and other people.

This all sounds very good for people who tend to be positive, optimistic, and grateful. What if we don't naturally gravitate to experiencing this positive emotion? Being mindful, without judgment, of how you generally experience life may actually turn into a starting point for practicing gratitude. The brain has the ability to change neural connections based on different experiences, thoughts, emotions; this ability is known as neuroplasticity. "We can recruit the power of neuroplasticity to repair damaged connections and create new, more satisfying patterns in our everyday lives" (Siegel, 2011, p. 44). Therefore, when we change the way we think or feel about people, experiences, and so on, we are able to rewire our brain and change the way our brain responds to those experiences. Neuroplasticity of the brain is a powerful capability that allows us to heal, grow, and evolve.

Now that we understand that we are able to teach ourselves new ways of responding to experiences and train our brain to be more grateful, a few suggestions by Robert Emmons (2010) to cultivate gratitude are included in this paragraph and the following paragraph. Emmons's first recommendation is to keep a gratitude journal. Take a few moments each day to think of something you are grateful for and write it down. It can be a personal accomplishment, an act of kindness you received, or something you experienced. Borysenko (2014) mentioned that if you think of just one new and different thing each day to be grateful for, you are exercising the neuroplasticity in your brain and rewiring your brain to experience more gratitude.

Second, Emmons (2010) says that making a *promise* to yourself to practice gratitude increases the likelihood of actually doing it. He suggests writing a note somewhere that says something like, "I promise to practice gratitude every day" (page number?). Seeing this message serves as a constant reminder and reinforces the practice. He also suggests paying attention to your five senses. "Through our senses, we gain an appreciation of what it means to be human and of what an incredible miracle it is to be alive. Seen through the lens of gratitude, the human body is not only a miraculous construction, but also a gift" (page number?). Some examples of opportunities to express gratitude when using our senses may include smelling a fragrant flower, touching a soft pillow, or enjoying the taste of a piece of delicious fresh fruit.

On a personal note, I followed these practices and took them one step further. I created a website called www.gratefuloptimism.com and I posted a daily affirmation of gratitude for one year. I included photographs to enhance the affirmation of gratitude. Looking back, I am grateful that I took the time and energy to create this website. People still thank me for this gift. The beauty of expressing gratitude is that once you start, it becomes easier and easier, and it feels really good. If you write down just one thing that you are grateful for every day, at the end of one month, you will have thirty things that you are grateful for, and after one year, you will have 365 documented instances of gratitude (Swisa, 2013, pp. 35–36).

Cognitively-Based Compassion Training (CBCT) discusses an additional approach for practicing gratitude. This approach involves expanding our circle of gratitude. It begins by feeling grateful for our caregivers and loved ones. We then include appreciation for people who have been helpful to us in other ways, like our teachers and other mentors. We continue to expand this circle to include benefits we have received from strangers. (Negi, 2015). If we think about everything that we experience in an ordinary day, we begin to realize the thousands of people who have contributed to our well-being. How many people helped put a roof over our head? There were contractors, carpenters, electricians, plumbers, city inspectors, and so on. How many people help provide electricity and water to our residence? How many people contribute to the infrastructure of our town or city including roads, snow removal, garbage removal? How many people contributed to providing the food we eat? When we begin to consider the "intended or unintended kindness of others" (Negi, 2015), we have thousands of reasons to be grateful.

In conclusion, I would like to share some thoughts by David Steindl-Rast, a Benedictine monk who has spoken publicly about how gratitude enriches our lives. The particular talk used in this chapter is from a TED Talk given in 2013, titled "Want To Be Happy? Be Grateful." Steindl-Rast calls gratitude "a real gift." Gratitude isn't something that we can buy; it's something that we are given by a person or an experience. We can live gratefully "by experiencing, by becoming aware that every moment…. is a gift…Open all your senses for this wonderful richness that is given to us. There is no end to it, and that is what life is all about, to enjoy what is given to us."

This is the beauty and magic of gratitude; it is an infinite source of positive emotion and positive energy. The more we appreciate our lives, the better we feel. The better we feel, the better those with whom we interact will feel. The better those with whom we interact feel, the better those with whom they interact will feel, and so forth. When we begin to understand the tremendous impact that expressing a little gratitude and appreciation may have on another person, we begin to understand the ease with which we can make a positive difference in this world. We are giving ourselves and everyone we encounter a gift that leads them toward better physical health, better psychological health, and better interpersonal relationships.

Thank Activity

The Gratitude Activity

This activity is appropriate for all levels of language learners. This can be used as one activity. However, it is best when participants are able to spend a few minutes each day focusing on gratitude so that it becomes an ongoing part of their personal and professional lives.

Goal: to experience the benefits of gratitude and incorporate that practice into their lives.

1. Introduce the concept of gratitude. Write the word "gratitude" on the board. Give participants an opportunity to come up to the board and write one word that they associate with gratitude.
2. Discuss the words that participants wrote on the board, including any new vocabulary.
3. Ask participants to share with a partner if they practice gratitude regularly. Why or why not?
4. Show the TED Talk by Louie Schwartzberg (2011) titled "Nature. Beauty. Gratitude."
5. Divide into pairs or small groups to share impressions about the video.
6. Share impressions with the whole group.
7. Discuss the benefits of practicing gratitude.
8. If possible, give each participant a gift of a small journal. If that isn't possible, ask participants to designate a part of their notebook as a gratitude journal.
9. Tell participants that they should write down one new and different thing that they are grateful for every day for one month.

10. After the participants are using the journal, you might decide to begin or end each session by asking participants to share one thought of gratitude.

11. After participants have at least ten entries, participants will create a gratitude mobile. The materials needed are flexible and may include colorful index cards (or card stock cut into smaller pieces), scissors, glue, colored markers, clothes hangers, magazines (for decoration, if desired), and string, yarn, or ribbon.

12. Participants will write each thought of gratitude on separate index cards. They can decorate the cards with glitter, pictures, drawings, or other art. They will create a mobile with the cards by connecting the cards, using a piece of string or ribbon, to a clothes hanger.

13. If possible, participants can hang the mobiles in their work space. If that isn't possible, participants may take them home as a gratitude reminder.

Closing Reflection

1. In closing, ask participants if they liked the activity. Why or why not?

2. Ask participants if they think practicing gratitude is beneficial. Why or why not?

3. Ask participants if they would like to continue expressing gratitude on an ongoing basis.

4. Have participants stand in a circle and share an expression of gratitude.

Chapter 6

Hearten

Let us always meet each other with a smile
for a smile is the beginning of love.

—*Mother Teresa*

Merriam-Webster defines "hearten" as "to cause someone to feel more cheerful or hopeful." *Merriam-Webster* includes "to give heart to" as a definition for the word "hearten." When we give our heart to something, we put a lot of feeling and effort into it. The heart is often used as the symbol for love. When we put a lot of effort into something and add love, we have a lot of positive energy flowing. Love is the ultimate positive feeling. Compassion, acceptance, forgiveness, and gratitude, discussed in previous chapters, are emotions that express the positive feeling of love for ourselves and other people. A more inclusive meaning of hearten, which incorporates both definitions while including love—is to give from our hearts with love in all our endeavors and contribute to the well-being of others. Contributing to the well-being of others includes promoting love, joy, laughter, and happiness. When we practice this as part of our daily lives, we are incorporating heart into everything we experience. This is the essence of love. This is also the essence of this chapter. A loving-kindness meditation activity is included at the end of the chapter.

Opening our hearts is the key to giving and receiving love. The Greeks spoke of four different kinds of love. The first type of love, *philia*, is affectionate love, such as the love of friends (*Wikipedia*, Greek words for love). Most of us are comfortable with affectionate love, especially because there is an element of choice involved; we *choose* our friends. Consequently, it is natural to feel love and affection for our friends and wish them happiness and well-being. The second type of love, *eros*, is passionate love, such as the love between two intimate partners. This type of love may transcend to a nonphysical level of love as well. The third type of love, *storge*, is familial love, such as the love of parents for children and vice versa. Although we may experience negative feelings toward our family, there is generally an underlying feeling of unconditional love for our family, or at least some members of our family. I would also include the love of animals—especially pets—in this category because most of us feel a sense of unconditional love for our pets. The last type of love, *agape*, is universal love, such as the love between a divine presence and humans, which may be expressed through good will and benevolence. While this may not be completely in keeping with the original Greek definition, I would include the love of nature and self-love in this category of universal love. Self-love is expressed through compassion, acceptance, forgiveness, and gratitude for ourselves as discussed in previous chapters. Universal love is an all-encompassing love and therefore includes the other three types of love within it. Universal love is the heart-opening love that allows us to love everyone, including ourselves, with nonjudgment, compassion, acceptance, and forgiveness.

As with other topics we've explored, self-love is not always easy. As a matter of fact, many of us may find self-love the most challenging of all, yet it is essential to our health and well-being. Robert Holden, PhD, author of *Loveability* (2013), wrote that "the quality of your relationship with yourself determines your relationship with everything else" (p. 45). Holden defines self-love as "a loving attitude from which positive actions arise that benefit you and others" (p. 49). "A basic fear for many of us is 'I'm not loveable' or 'I'm not enough'" (p. 73). "Whenever you don't feel loveable it's because you are judging yourself" (p. 55). Holden goes on to say that "the essence of who we are is always loveable" (p. 122). Holden's statements coincide with many of the topics we have discussed thus far. By practicing mindfulness and paying attention without judgment, we treat ourselves with compassion, acceptance, and forgiveness, and we begin the heart-opening journey toward self-love. Once we are able to open our hearts with nonjudgment, compassion, acceptance, forgiveness, and gratitude in the expression of self-love, we are able to expand this love to include others. This is the moment when we are able to give from our heart and experience the positive emotion of giving and receiving love.

One way to give and receive love and hearten the lives of others is through the experience of joy. Joy is an emotion that promotes physical and emotional well-being. Laughter is one way to experience joy. The physical and psychological effects are similar to the effects of gratitude. Dr. Lee Berk, of Loma Linda School of Medicine, has spent years researching the positive effects of laughter. He has concluded that laughter *is* the best medicine. He discussed his findings in three interviews with Sanjay Gupta of CNN and others, available on YouTube (https://www.youtube.com/watch?v=nt0QrmATtfk). Like gratitude, laughter decreases stress hormones, which improves our immune system. Furthermore, laughter increases our endorphin levels, especially when we do this for thirty minutes three or four times week. Endorphins are sometimes called the "happy" hormone, often associated with exercise. Dr. Berk performed a laughter study with heart attack patients who were divided into two groups, one that watched comedies for thirty minutes every day for one year and one that did not. After one year, only 8 percent of the group that practiced laughter regularly suffered from a second heart attack, but 42 percent of the nonlaughter group suffered a second heart attack (Berk, 2012) However, Berk noted that humor that is demeaning or derogatory doesn't elicit the same positive benefits (Berk, 2012) because this type of humor contains an underlying message of hostility. In order for humor to be beneficial, the humor must elicit positive feelings. Some examples of humor that is supportive and positive include movies by Mel Brooks, such as *Young Frankenstein* (1974); movies by Monty Python, such as *Monty Python and the Holy Grail* (1975); *Romy and Michelle's High School Reunion* (1997); *The Gods Must Be Crazy* (1980); *Trading Places* (1983); Disney's *Aladdin* (1992); and *Patch Adams* (1998), to name a few. Some television shows that are positively funny include *The Big Bang Theory* (2007–), *Saturday Night Live* (1975–), and *Seinfeld* (1989–1998). If none of these are appealing, search for other shows on the Internet. Although I haven't included an activity at the end of the chapter on laughter, an English Language learning activity might use one or more of these movies and television shows as an opportunity to explore the many health benefits of laughter and humor, while practicing speaking and listening.

Madan Kataria (2011), a physician and the founder of Laughter Yoga International, has discovered additional benefits. Laughter yoga combines laughter exercises with yoga breathing. Like other physical exercise, laughter yoga increases the net supply of oxygen to the body and the brain, which makes us feel more energetic. Furthermore, the body is not able to distinguish between real laughter and fake laughter, so our body reaps the same physical and emotional benefits. In addition to the physical health benefits, laughter yoga provides emotional and social benefits as well. Regular laughter contributes to a more positive attitude and outlook. Kataria (2011) concludes by saying that laughing with people creates positive social connections, which in turn, improves the quality of relationships with other people. This in turn reduces defensiveness and breaks down social and emotional barriers among people. When our defenses are lower, and we feel better, our hearts are more open to the positive aspects of life, including love.

The concept of universal love includes all of the other aspects of love and positive emotions within it. While practicing mindfulness and nonjudgment, and remembering the importance of compassion, acceptance, forgiveness, and gratitude, we are paving the way for happier, more joyful lives for ourselves and other people. Deepak Chopra (2014) said, "Love is what we are in our essence, and the more we feel in our hearts, the more it will be brought to us."

With that in our minds and our hearts, let's all think about opportunities to change our negative emotions into the positive emotions we truly want to embrace and make our lives and the lives of all people, more loving, more peaceful and more joyful.

All you need is love.

—*John Lennon and Paul McCartney*

Hearten Activity

These are suggested activities and may be modified for the needs of your participants. This loving-kindness meditation activity is divided into three parts. The introduction familiarizes participants with vocabulary and the topic. The listening phase is the loving-kindness meditation. The post phase is the opportunity to reflect on the activity, including the exploration of next steps.

This meditation is based on a combination of the loving-kindness meditation of Sharon Salzberg, author of *Lovingkindness* (1995), and Jack Kornfield, author of *A Path With Heart* (1993). Sharon Salzberg has a guided loving-kindness mediation on YouTube at https://www.youtube.com/watch?v=W3uLqt69VyI. I have recorded my own version available on Vocaroo at http://vocaroo.com/i/s1Avi8vG22op.

Goal: to practice meditation and experience the feeling of loving-kindness.

Introduction:

1. Begin by writing the word "loving-kindness" on the board. Ask participants what the word means. What feelings do they associate with this concept?
2. Review the definitions of mindfulness and meditation. Make sure to include the concepts of paying attention, being compassionate, and being accepting. Ask participants what they remember about the previous meditation activity, particularly posture and breath.

3. Discuss any other vocabulary that may be needed, such as interconnectedness.
4. Ask participants to think about and discuss in pairs the following four phrases.
    a. May I be safe and peaceful.
    b. May I be happy and healthy.
    c. May I be filled with loving-kindness.
    d. May I give and receive appreciation today.

    Tell them that these four phrases will be used in this meditation and that this is a meditation on loving-kindness.

Listening Phase:

I have included a recording of the meditation as well at http://vocaroo.com/i/s1Avi8vG22op.

[Begin meditation]

This meditation focuses on loving-kindness. We will pay attention to opening our hearts so that we may create a deeper sense of personal well-being and love for ourselves and for all beings.

Find a comfortable position either sitting in a chair or on the floor. Keep your back straight and shoulders broad. Place your hands in your lap or on your thighs, palms facing up in a relaxed position. Gently close your eyes. Notice any tension you may feel in your body. Take three slow breaths. As you exhale, release any tension you may be feeling. And relax.

We begin this meditation by feeling loving-kindness toward ourselves. Think of one thing you like about yourself, a particular quality, some part of yourself that you have respect for, or something good that you've done for yourself or others. Perhaps it's a time when you've been generous, or you've been careful, or you've been honest—anything that you can think of.

If you can't think of anything that you've done or that you like about yourself, rest your mind and think about your wish to be happy. You, like all human beings, simply want to be happy.

As you continue with this meditation, remember to take slow deep breaths, inhale and exhale. Breathe in. Breathe out.

Meditate on these words as you practice loving-kindness toward yourself.

May I be safe and peaceful.
May I be happy and healthy.
May I be filled with loving-kindness.
May I give and receive appreciation today.

Use these phrases or whatever phrases are most meaningful to you. Let each phrase emerge from your heart and simply connect with it without trying to force any special feeling or make anything special happen.

May I be safe and peaceful.
May I be happy and healthy.
May I be filled with loving-kindness.
May I give and receive appreciation today.

Develop a rhythm that feels comfortable to you as you repeat the phrases. Take your time. Give yourself space. Let the phrases emerge naturally while you continue taking slow deep breaths.

May I be safe and peaceful.
May I be happy and healthy.
May I be filled with loving-kindness.
May I give and receive appreciation today.

The next expansion of our loving-kindness meditation includes someone who has been good to you, helped you, taken care of you, been generous to you…someone who is inspiring to you and has taught you to be loving and compassionate. This person is known as the benefactor in the traditional loving-kindness meditation.

If someone comes to mind, try to visualize them by seeing an image of them in your mind or maybe say their name silently to yourself. Get a feeling for them as though they were here in front of you.

Remember the good that they've done for you and their good qualities. Begin offering them loving-kindness through the phrases we mentioned earlier.

May you be safe and peaceful.
May you be happy and healthy.
May you be filled with loving-kindness.
May you give and receive appreciation today.

If there is no one who comes to mind as a benefactor, simply continue to focus on yourself and give the feeling of loving-kindness to yourself while you remember to take slow deep breaths.

We further open our hearts to include a friend. If you think of a friend, visualize him or her by seeing an image of your friend in your mind or saying your friend's name silently to yourself. Bring your friend here and include him or her in this meditation of friendship and loving-kindness. Try to wish for your friend what you have wished for yourself. Remember that this person also wants to be happy.

May you be safe and peaceful.
May you be happy and healthy.
May you be filled with loving-kindness.
May you give and receive appreciation today.

And we continue to take slow deep breaths.

We now expand our circle of loving-kindness to include all people everywhere. As we think about and appreciate the interconnectedness of all life, we send this message of universal loving-kindness to all life.

May all beings be safe and peaceful.
May all beings be happy and healthy.
May all beings be filled with loving-kindness.
May all beings give and receive appreciation today.

And we continue to take slow deep breaths—inhale and exhale.

May all beings be safe and peaceful.
May all beings be happy and healthy.
May all beings be filled with loving-kindness.
May all beings give and receive appreciation today.

When you're ready, gently open your eyes as you continue to be open to the power of loving-kindness throughout the day and every day.

[End meditation]

Post Phase

The post phase is the opportunity for reflection. Discussion may include any combination of writing, reading, speaking, and listening individually, in pairs, small groups, or with the whole group. The questions on the following page may help facilitate the discussion.

1. This is an opportunity to for participants to reflect on this meditation. Ask them a few questions about this experience. Here are some suggestions.
    a. What did you like about this meditation?
    b. What was challenging?
    c. Did you experience any thoughts of discomfort?
    d. How was this meditation different from the breath meditation or the self-compassion meditation?
    e. Do you feel different after this meditation? Why or why not?
    f. Do you feel more loving-kindness toward yourself? Toward others? Why or why not?
2. If you are not in a circle, ask your participants to stand or sit in a circle.
    a. Go around the circle and ask participants to share one thing that they discovered that they like about themselves or someone they know.
    b. Close by asking how they are feeling at this moment.

Closing activity:

If it feels appropriate, it might be nice to end with a song that contributes to feelings of loving-kindness like Stevie Wonder's "I Just Called to Say I Love You" (https://www.youtube.com/watch?v=QwOU3bnuU0k), and allow participants to sing and dance and spread the feeling of loving-kindness and add some good cheer.

Chapter 7

Engage

Interconnectedness is a fundamental principle of nature.

—*Jon Kabat-Zinn*

Now that we have explored many positive emotions, it is time to integrate them into all aspects of our lives, including our relationships with others and with nature, and realize the depth and breadth of our interconnectedness. To *engage* means to be involved or participate. Participation and mindfulness are closely related. When we participate in any activity with mindfulness, we begin to experience our connection with ourselves, our surroundings, and other people on a deeper level. According to Siegel (2011), human beings are "equipped with a mammalian limbic region of the brain" (p. 17). The limbic area of the brain is the reason that humans and other mammals form emotional attachments with one another (p. 17). Because of this, human beings are "hardwired to connect with one another" (p. 17). Forming connections with others, therefore, is an integral part of our existence. When we begin to feel self-love and other positive emotions, we are able to extend these emotions to others and feel a true connection with other people. We are then able to begin to expand those connections and experience the interconnectedness of all things. Realizing this sense of interconnectedness reduces our feelings of separateness and aloneness and increases our feelings of well-being and happiness (p. 259). Our sense of interconnectedness is augmented as our awareness expands. Expanded awareness results from engaging in mindfulness and acts of kindness. Engaging in mindfulness and acts of kindness promotes feelings of happiness and well-being. The workplace or classroom is a wonderful microcosm in which to explore our interconnectedness. Activities to enhance this exploration are included.

Awareness of our interconnectedness is expressed through mindfulness and acts of kindness. As previously discussed, mindfulness is paying attention in the present moment without judgment and with acceptance (Kabat-Zinn, 1994, p. 4). As with all experiences, engaging in the practice of mindfulness is an essential step toward experiencing our interconnectedness. When we interact with nonjudgment and acceptance, we are opening the door to experience all interactions with a greater sense of well-being and happiness. Acts of kindness include all acts that promote a sense of well-being in ourselves, other people, and our environment. Acts of kindness include topics previously discussed such as compassion, acceptance, forgiveness, and gratitude. Acts of generosity also contribute to our greater sense of happiness, well-being, and interconnectedness.

Practicing random acts of kindness and generosity positively affect our level of happiness. Sonja Lyubomirski, Ken Sheldon, and Dave Schkade (2005) conducted research at the University of California–Riverside on the "factors that determine our level of happiness" (http://greatergood.berkeley.edu/article/item/happiness_for_a_lifetime). They found that 10 percent of our happiness is based on life circumstances and 50 percent is based on our genetic inclination for happiness. The other 40 percent is based on our "behavior and daily activities" (Lyubomirski, 2010). If 40 percent of our level of happiness is based on our behavior, then Lyubomirski et al. hypothesized that we have the ability to consciously affect our level of happiness.

> In one of these studies, we asked college participants to do five acts of kindness per week over a period of six weeks. Each week, we asked one group of participants to do all five of their acts of kindness in one day; another group of participants could spread out their acts of kindness over the entire week. And a third group of participants (a control group) didn't do anything at all (Lyubomirski et al., 2005).

This study found that the participants who performed five acts of kindness in a single day exhibited the greatest boost to their personal happiness (Lyubomirski et al., 2005). One reason for this may be that we feel better about ourselves when we consider ourselves to be kind and generous (Lyubomirski et al., 2005). This may promote a pattern of kindness and generosity that permeates other interpersonal interactions as well, thereby expanding the circle of kindness. When we feel better about ourselves, we treat others with more kindness, compassion, and acceptance, among other things. They in turn may begin to model this behavior with others, and so on, and so on.

There have been other studies that demonstrate the positive effects of generosity on our health and well-being. In a 2006 study, Moll and colleagues at the National Institutes of Health found that when people give to charities, it activates regions of the brain associated with pleasure, social connection, and trust, creating a "warm glow" effect.

Scientists discovered that altruistic behavior releases endorphins in the brain, producing the positive feeling known as the "helper's high" (p. 15623). The helper's high is that heightened sense of well-being we feel after helping another person or cause. The helper's high also promotes the perpetuation of generosity; we want to continue to find opportunities to experience feeling good by being generous.

As with other positive emotions, giving to others has positive effects on our health. Oman, Thoresen, and McMahon (1999) discovered that elderly people who volunteered for "two or more organizations, were 44 percent less likely to die over a five-year period than those who didn't volunteer" (p. 301). Being generous has been shown to reduce stress as well (Marsh & Suttie, 2010). They write, "In a 2006 study by Rachel Piferi of Johns Hopkins University and Kathleen Lawler of the University of Tennessee, people who provided social support to others had lower blood pressure than participants who didn't, suggesting a direct physiological benefit to those who give of themselves." Stephen Post, professor of medicine at University of New York at Stony Brook, concluded that giving to others also promotes a greater sense of cooperation and connectedness (Post, 2005, p. 70). The study of positive psychology has determined that feeling connected to something beyond our "personal self" makes us feel better about ourselves (Siegel, 2011, p. 259). As discussed previously, positive social interactions also contribute to our physical and emotional health. Being kind and generous encourages us to perceive other people more positively (Marsh & Suttie, 2010). This in turn contributes to our sense of well-being because we are focusing on positive rather than negative aspects of our interpersonal connections. In addition, when we realize that our acts of generosity help others, we are more apt to perpetuate the practice. Not surprisingly, giving also "evokes gratitude" (Marsh & Suttie, 2010). The act of giving and receiving promotes feelings of gratitude in both the giver and the recipient (Marsh & Suttie, 2010) because it demonstrates our connection with others. Many of the benefits of gratitude have been discussed in chapter 5, particularly as it relates to physical health, psychological well-being, and interpersonal relationships.

Any discussion of our interconnectedness must also include our interconnectedness with our ecosystem. Goleman, Bennett, and Barlow (2013), have applied theories of social and emotional intelligence to include ecological intelligence. "While social and emotional intelligence extend participants' abilities to see from another's perspective, empathize, and show concern, ecological intelligence applies these capacities to an understanding of natural systems and melds cognitive skills with empathy for all of life." Goleman et al. have developed an ecoliteracy program to raise awareness of our interconnectedness and interdependence through education. Ecoliteracy integrates emotional, social, and ecological intelligence into educational practices. When children begin to feel a greater connection with our ecosystem, they begin to understand the intricacy of our web of interconnectedness. Goleman et al. discuss several ways to cultivate our ecoliteracy in the group room and beyond.

The first involves expanding our feeling of compassion to include our natural environment. One way to do this is to grow plants or vegetables in the classroom. In this way, participants gain an appreciation for the effort involved in sustaining plant life.

The second way involves realizing that in order for our planet to thrive, we must work together as a community. By studying the behavior of plants and animals, participants begin to understand the interconnectedness of people and communities as well (Goleman et al., 2013). Using the local community as a starting point for this exploration provides a framework that demonstrates immediacy and relevance to participants.

The third way is to "make the invisible visible" (Goleman et al., 2013). The Internet provides countless opportunities for participants to see areas of the world they might not normally see. This helps participants widen their circle of compassion to include more people, places, flora, and fauna. The more participants connect with other people and ecosystems, the more they understand the depth and breadth of our interconnectedness.

The last way is to view nature as our teacher. Nature demonstrates the complex interdependency of all organisms. Goleman et al. recommend studying the local ecosystem as a starting point for understanding our interconnectedness. The local ecosystem provides a framework that is immediately accessible to participants. While the focus discussed by Goleman et al. is not specifically on personal well-being, based on the previous discussion of acts of kindness and generosity, it would seem logical that practicing compassion toward our ecosystem and our community also results in a greater sense of personal well-being.

We have discussed how helping others and feeling connected to others positively affects our emotional and physical health and well-being. In his book, *Mindsight* (2011), Daniel Siegel discusses the "Triangle of Well-Being" that integrates "relationships, mind, and brain" to form this sense of well-being (p. 267).

The *Triangle of Well-Being* reveals three aspects of our lives. *Relationships, Mind,* and *Brain* form three mutually influencing points of the *Triangle of Well-Being*. *Relationships* are how energy and information is shared as we connect and communicate with one another. *Brain* refers to the physical mechanism through which this energy and information flows. *Mind* is a process that regulates the flow of energy and information. Rather than dividing our lives into three separate parts, the Triangle actually represents three dimensions of one system of energy and information flow (Siegel, 2011, p. 267).

When our mind, brain, and relationships are integrated and working together, "well-being" ensues (p. 267.). For example, the type of integration that leads to well-being might occur as a result of an interaction with a loved one. When we are able to connect with that loved one in a way that feels positive to us and the other person, we experience a sense of well-being. These are moments when our thoughts, actions, and relationships work together and "flow," resulting in a greater sense of well-being.

Practicing mindfulness and performing acts of kindness for others are opportunities to perpetuate these moments of well-being and integrate them into our daily lives. As mentioned earlier, the limbic area of the brain hardwires humans to connect with others (Siegel, 2011, p. 17). Therefore, it seems logical that when we experience greater awareness and mindfulness of our interconnectedness, we experience a greater sense of well-being. The cycle of well-being on the following page illustrates the connections that lead to a greater sense of well-being. The cycle of well-being results from heightened awareness as we engage in positive actions and feelings of connection. In the cycle of well-being, these elements are interconnected and interrelated. Awareness is present and part of everything we experience. Awareness is our state of *being*. Awareness raises the quality of our actions and increases the realization of the intricacies of our interconnectedness. Actions, such as mindfulness and acts of kindness, are what we *do* to promote interconnectedness and raise our level of awareness. Interconnectedness becomes more apparent—experienced with our *senses* as a result of our actions and heightened awareness. Awareness, actions, and interconnectedness work together to promote feelings of happiness and well-being. Figure 2 illustrates this interrelated cycle of well-being.

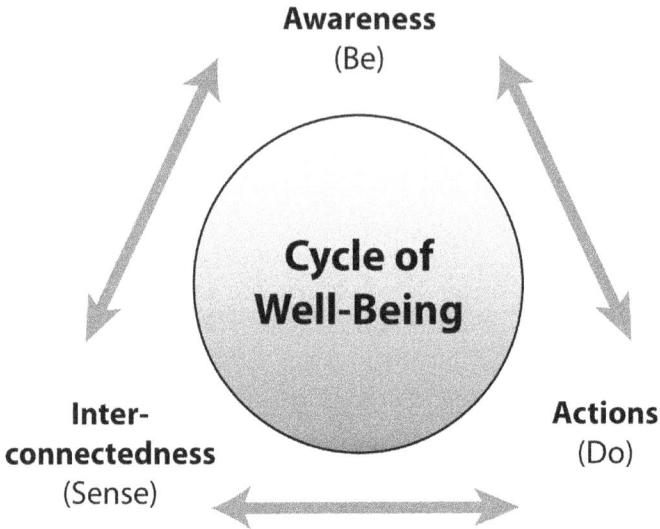

Figure 2. Cycle of Well-Being (Swisa, 2015)

All feelings, actions, and sensations that promote well-being in ourselves and others contribute to both our individual and our collective sense of well-being and interconnectedness. Feeling compassion for others connects us to one another because we are mindful of the universal reality that we all want to alleviate our suffering and experience more joy in our lives. Accepting each situation as it is connects us to one another because we interact with greater ease, greater mindfulness, and greater nonjudgment. Forgiveness connects us to one another because as we let go of negative emotions, we are able to break down barriers and allow for more meaningful interpersonal relationships. Gratitude connects us to one another because as we appreciate our lives more, we are able to share that appreciation with others. Generosity connects us to one another because when we give of ourselves, we experience the positive effects of that generosity on our lives and the lives of others. These are all elements of universal love. When we engage in these acts of kindness with love, we expand the circle of our interconnectedness and continue the journey toward greater health, well-being, happiness, and wholeness for ourselves, all living beings, and the planet.

Engage Activities

This activity has three parts: an opening community builder, the main activity, and a closing reflective activity. All three activities revolve around experiencing our interconnectedness. The activities may be done separately, if time is limited. As with all activities, these are suggestions. Feel free to modify them according to your participants' needs.

Activity 1: Human Knot

This activity is a community builder. After you give the instructions, it is up to the participants to untwist the knot through communication, cooperation, and teamwork. Participants need to stand very close to one another, so it is important that participants feel comfortable with this. If any participants are not comfortable holding hands and touching, or they have any disabilities that make participating difficult, there are two additional roles that may be included. The first is that of instructor. The instructor tells the participants what to try when the participants are not sure what to do. It is probably best to have only one instructor. The second is that of observer. There may be as many observers as needed. The observers watch the process and discuss their observations at the end.

1. If there are any observers, provide them with some items to notice. You might want to hand these questions out so that they can write down some key thoughts. Some sample questions might be
   a. Pay attention to the language that people are using. Are they communicating in English or their native language?
   b. Is one person giving instructions, or are multiple people giving instructions?

c. What happens when they don't know what to do?

d. Was the mood of the group cooperative?

e. Were they having fun?

f. Did they seem to be frustrated?

g. Are there any overall observations about the process? Did it go smoothly? What was challenging?

2. Ask the remaining participants to stand in a circle, shoulder to shoulder. The optimal number of participants in one circle is between eight and twelve. If the group has sixteen or more participants, it may be helpful to create two circles. If there are two circles, make sure there is plenty of space for both circles.

3. Remind participants that they need to communicate in English only. It might be helpful to write that on the board as well.

4. Ask participants to shake and hold hands with someone in the circle who isn't standing next to them. Tell them to continue to hold on to that hand. *Don't let go.*

5. Ask participants to shake hands with a different person, using their other hand, and continue holding on to that hand with someone who isn't standing next to them. Tell them to continue to hold on to that hand as well. Don't let go.

6. Remind participants that they need to keep holding on to one another's hands. Don't let go.

7. Now, let them know that the goal is to unravel themselves and end up in a circle.

8. To achieve this goal, participants may need to step over, under, and around arms, legs, and bodies.

9. Let participants solve this puzzle on their own. If there is an instructor for the activity, remind him or her that it is OK to help.

10. This is a very participatory activity.

11. Sometimes participants may want to try a second time if they had difficulties. If time permits, feel free to let them try again.
12. When they are done, ask them to reflect on the activity.
    a. First, ask the observers to share what they noticed.
    b. What did they like about the activity?
    c. What was important during the activity?
    d. Did they have to work together?
    e. What did this activity demonstrate about working together?
    f. What did they learn?

Activity 2: The Interconnectedness of Everything

This activity demonstrates the depth and breadth of our interconnectedness and how we experience that in our daily lives.

Goal: to realize the intricacies of our interconnectedness with one another and the natural world.

1. Write the word "interconnectedness" on the board.
2. Ask participants to talk to their neighbors about what this means.
3. Discuss as a group.
4. Review the meanings of mindfulness and nonjudgment with the group.
5. Write the word "brainstorm" on the board.
6. Ask participants to talk to their neighbors about what this word means.
7. Discuss as a group. Remind participants that brainstorming involves a free flow of ideas, with no judgment and no censoring. Everything is acceptable.

8. Divide the group into small groups of four or five.
9. Give each group a different topic to explore. Write a different topic on each index card. Hand one index card to each group. Here are a few examples of topics:
   a. T-shirt
   b. Bicycle
   c. Apple
   d. Book
   e. Computer
   f. Table
10. Remind participants to be mindful during the activity.
11. Ask each group to brainstorm and think about every person, place, object, animal, or plant that has been involved in getting that item to you.
12. Tell them to write their ideas on a large sheet of paper or newsprint.
13. After a few minutes of brainstorming, have them work together to create a visual (like a diagram or collage) that depicts all the people, places, objects, or other entities that were involved in getting that item to you.
14. Depending on time, you might have each group present its findings to the whole group. If time is short, participants can travel as a group and view one another's work.
15. After participants have had a chance to view one another's work, have them sit in a circle for the closing reflection.
    a. Ask participants to share something that they noticed during this activity. This could be a thought, feeling, or an interaction.
    b. Ask participants if it was difficult to think of who and what might have been involved in getting that item to them.

c. Ask participants, "How many people, places, or things were involved in getting that item to you?"
d. Ask participants to discuss what this activity demonstrates about our interconnectedness.
e. Ask participants how that makes them feel.
f. Close by going around the circle and having each participant share something he or she learned from this activity.

Activity 3: The Interconnectedness of Our Group

This is a nice closing activity. It can be used to conclude this unit on interconnectedness, or it can also be used as a closing activity at the end of a semester, or whenever there is the need for closure that promotes a sense of connection.

1. Bring a ball of yarn or string.
2. Have participants stand in a circle.
3. Take the end of the yarn and hold on to it.
4. Roll the ball of yarn across the floor. Have another participant hold on to the yarn so that the strand of yarn feels slightly taut between you and that participant.
5. Have the participant roll the ball of yarn to another participant and make sure that the strand of yarn feels slightly taut between those two participants.
6. Continue until all of the participants are holding on to the yarn.
7. Remind participants to continue to hold on to the yarn.
8. Have all the participants lightly pull on the yarn and ask them what they notice.

9. Ask participants what they think this yarn represents.
10. Ask participants to share a way that they feel connected to other members of the group.
11. Ask each participant to share something they are grateful for.

Understand

Seek first to understand, then to be understood.

—*STEPHEN COVEY*

We have discussed the value of mindfulness, nonjudgment, acceptance, gratitude, and generosity. There is one additional ingredient that is necessary for positive interpersonal relationships: understanding. Understanding is another lens through which we experience connections with people. There are two aspects of understanding that will be discussed in this chapter. The first involves direct, individual understanding, which happens when we are interacting with another person in a dialogue. The second involves cultural understanding, which happens when we are seeking to understand how culture influences our values and customs.

The use of language is essential in order to communicate effectively with the goal to understand in both of these instances. Listening with mindfulness and nonjudgment is always very important, especially when interacting with one other person in a dialogue. Active listening techniques help facilitate this process. Some active listening guidelines and techniques are included in this chapter as well. Two activities are included in this chapter; the first activity focuses on individual understanding, using active listening techniques, and the other focuses on cultural understanding.

Listening is an important skill when communicating with other people in order to understand their point of view. Listening to understand is a skill that needs to be learned and practiced in order to develop and improve (Curran, 1978, p. 65). In *The Seven Habits of Highly Effective People*, Stephen Covey (1989) discusses "empathic listening" and the four "developmental stages" associated with it (p. 248). The first stage is to listen to the speaker and to "mimic" back what the listener hears (p. 248). In this stage, the listener repeats what the speaker said, more or less verbatim. In the second stage, the listener "rephrases" what the speaker said (p. 249). Covey refers to these first two levels as focused solely on the verbal level of communication (p. 249). In the third stage, the listener begins to listen for the "feeling" that the speaker is conveying (p. 249). The fourth stage is where the listener is able to both rephrase and reflect the feeling of the speaker. The fourth stage of empathic listening is where the listener is able to "understand their paradigm...understand how they feel" (p. 240). This is a moment when the listener is able to listen and accurately convey the speaker's intention, including emotions, without interjecting personal opinions or values. This is a moment when the speaker feels understood.

Like Covey, Curran (1986) views listening for understanding as a skill that develops with time and experience. In *Understanding: An Essential Ingredient in Human Belonging*, Curran discusses the type of communication necessary to experience understanding. He focuses on the importance of listening with nonjudgment and acceptance on the listener's part so that the speaker feels safe to explore his or her thoughts and actions (p.52). The "sole concern" of the listener is to respond accurately to the truth of the speaker's "inner world, as [the speaker] sees it" (p. 54), without interjecting his or her personal values (p. 59). When this is done in a manner that is helpful to the speaker, the speaker feels understood. This sense of being understood is what might be referred to as an aha moment, a moment of clarity and greater awareness for the speaker, resulting in a changed inner view for that individual (p. 53). This may be a transformational moment for speakers (Covey, 1989, p. 251) because they feel heard, acknowledged, and accepted for who they are.

There is certain language when using empathic listening techniques that promotes greater understanding. These empathic listening techniques are commonly referred to as active listening techniques. Active listening involves focused listening while practicing mindfulness, non-judgment and empathy. Active listening uses statements like, "What I hear you saying is…" This is a way for the listener to rephrase what the speaker said to make sure that the listener understood the speaker. "Can you explain a little more?" is a way for the listener to ask for clarification. In general, asking questions for clarification lets the speaker know that the listener is trying to understand. "That sounds challenging" (or any adjective that describes feelings and emotions) is a way for the listener to demonstrate empathy. By asking questions like these and demonstrating empathy, the listener serves as a mirror for the speaker by reflecting what the listener hears. The listener is not trying to solve the speaker's problem or give advice (Curran, 1986, p. 50); the listener is trying to help the speaker gain greater insight and awareness into him- or herself and the situation.

Another important aspect of appropriate language when listening to understand is to keep the topic focused on the speaker. Covey (1989) mentions that even though we spend a great deal of our time communicating with other people, only 10 percent of that communication is verbal (p. 241). This means that verbal communication is only a small part of what we communicate when interacting with someone. The majority of our communication is based on nonverbal language, such as body language. Consequently, focused attention on the speaker is important. This includes maintaining eye contact and not doing other things while listening to the speaker. It also means that it is extremely important that we make sure that our verbal communication is as meaningful as possible. Using appropriate language when actively listening facilitates the process.

Paying attention to language usage is also important when exploring cultural understanding. In his book, *Teaching Culture*, Patrick Moran (2001) defines culture as "the evolving way of life of a group of persons, consisting of a shared set of practices associated with a shared set of products, based upon a shared set of perspectives on the world, and set within specific social contexts" (p. 24). An important word in this definition is "shared." Culture is based on the ways that these shared connections are carried out among people. Products are items that are produced such as tools, clothing, and buildings. Products also include educational systems, politics, and religion (p. 25). Practices consist of language, both verbal and nonverbal, and other forms of communication. (p. 25). Perspectives are the worldview, including beliefs and values (p. 25). Social contexts include groups or communities like gender, race, and socioeconomic class (p. 25). Lastly, Persons are the individuals that embody the culture (p. 25). Language is an important component of each of these. Moran states that "language is a product of the culture" (Moran, 2001, p. 35). Every culture uses words, phrases, and idioms in unique ways that portray various aspects of their culture. When we look more closely at language usage, we learn more about the culture. Moran mentions the French use of *tu* and *vous* to "establish roles and maintain relationships" (p. 35). The United States places importance on punctuality and success that is expressed through idioms such as "the early bird catches the worm."

Once we have identified the components of culture, we are able to explore elements that lead to greater cultural understanding. For the SIT Intercultural Communication for Language Teachers course in April 2014, I developed a three-week curriculum exploring the topic of cultural understanding. I simplified Moran's framework and reduced his five components of culture: products, practices, perspectives, communities, and people, to three components: customs, communities, and communication.

I taught the curriculum to a group of university participants from Costa Rica. The participants were divided into three groups and discussed each component. Some customs that they included were religious holidays, food, family traditions, and sports events. Communities included religious groups, educational groups, sports groups, and social groups. The communication component included methods of communication such as the Internet and mobile phones. These three concepts became the basis for the cultural inquiry that compared similarities and differences across cultures. The participants kept a daily journal in which they documented three similarities to and three differences between their home culture and the American culture. Participants engaged in other activities, such as creating a collage that documented these similarities and differences. The use of language was an important part of this inquiry. We discussed English idioms and compared them to idioms in their native language. Participants observed and reflected using all four skills. Through this process, participants learned about themselves, their cultures, and American culture. At the end of the three weeks, participants analyzed the data and answered the following question: "What do we learn by examining cultural similarities and differences?" The participants' response to that question was, "we learn open-mindedness, respect, and understanding." My personal hope is that understanding cultural similarities and differences leads to greater tolerance and peace in the world.

Using language as the vehicle for cultural and interpersonal exploration requires mindfulness. Mindfulness and understanding have many common qualities. As with mindfulness, understanding is a skill that improves with practice. As with mindfulness, greater awareness is a result of greater understanding. Like mindfulness, practicing nonjudgment is an important part of understanding. When we communicate with nonjudgment, we open the door for greater acceptance. Active listening skills are beneficial in this process. When a person feels understood and not judged, "he comes into a more harmonious relationship with himself through greater self-acceptance" (Curran, 1986, p. 60). Once a person feels greater self-acceptance, s/he is able to widen the circle of acceptance to include others. Jack Kornfield (1993) elaborates by saying, "In deep self-acceptance grows a compassionate understanding" (p. 312). When we create opportunities to practice greater acceptance and compassionate understanding, both culturally and interpersonally, we pave the way toward a more cooperative, peaceful existence.

Peace cannot be kept by force; it can only
be achieved through understanding.

—Albert Einstein

Understand Activities

There are two activities included. The first activity is suitable for intermediate English-language level and above. The second activity is suitable for all English-language levels. The first activity is to practice "empathic listening" (Covey, 1989, p. 248). The second activity explores cultural understanding. The activities may be done separately. As with all activities, these are suggestions. Feel free to modify them according to your participants' needs.

Activity 1: Interpersonal Understanding

This is an activity that focuses on communication especially through speaking and listening.

Goal: to practice active listening, which leads to greater interpersonal understanding.

1. Introduce key vocabulary and concepts such as understanding, active listening, acceptance, nonjudgment, rephrasing, and empathy.
2. Ask participants what they know about active listening. As discussed on pages 81–82 of this book, remind them of some of the important concepts of active listening, such as reflecting the speakers' ideas back to them. Listeners are not trying to solve the speakers' problems or give advice; they are trying to help the speakers gain greater insight and awareness into themselves and their situations. What statement might they use or questions

might they ask that demonstrate active listening? Some examples are on page 82.

   a. "What I hear you saying is…"

   b. "Can you explain a little more?"

   c. "That sounds…" (fill in the blank with an emotion)

3. Divide the group into groups of three.

4. Tell participants that each person will have an opportunity to be a speaker, a listener, and an observer.

5. Give participants a moment to think of a challenging situation that they are currently experiencing or have recently experienced. Let them know that they will be sharing this situation with their group, so it is important that they choose something that they are comfortable sharing.

6. Ask each group to decide who will speak about the first participant's situation.

7. Then ask the group to decide who is going to listen. Remind the listener that this time is for the speaker and to practice active listening. Remind the listener that it is important to listen with nonjudgment, ask for clarification, rephrase, and practice empathy.

8. The third person will be the observer. The observer's role is to pay attention to the dialogue. Is the listener practicing mindfulness and nonjudgment? Is the listener rephrasing and showing empathy? Does the speaker feel understood? What does the observer notice about nonverbal cues like body language, energy level, and intonation?

9. After ten to fifteen minutes, the three participants will spend a few minutes sharing what it was like for each of them. The speaker shares first, the listener shares second, and the observer shares last.

a. For the speaker: What did it feel like to talk about the situation? Did the speaker feel understood?

b. For the listener: What did it feel like to listen?

c. For the observer: What did you observe? Refer to the questions in number 8.

d. What were some of the challenges for each person?

10. Repeat steps 6 through 9 until each participant has had an opportunity to practice all three roles.

11. When each member has spoken, listened, and observed, ask them to share with one another a few highlights.

12. For a closing reflection, bring the whole group together in a circle.

a. Ask participants to share anything that was special about this activity.

b. Ask them to share how they might use this in their daily lives.

c. If the speaker felt understood, ask how it felt to be understood.

d. Ask them why it is important to feel understood.

e. Ask them to share something they learned.

Activity 2: Cultural Collage

This activity provides an opportunity for participants to explore cultural similarities and differences using visual aids as a tool. They will present their collage to the rest of the group when everyone is finished. This activity works particularly well in a multicultural group or a course that is taking place away from the participants' home countries.

Goal: to gain greater understanding of cultural differences and similarities.

Instructions:

1. Write the word "culture" on the board and ask participants what the word means. Include words like "customs," "communities," and "communication" in the definition.

2. Create a mind map with the participants, documenting various aspects of culture. (A mind map is a visual representation of concepts and how they relate to a central idea.) This might include subgroups and specific examples of the three concepts mentioned in step 1.

3. Ask participants to discuss, in small groups, aspects of their culture that are important to them.

4. Ask participants to discuss, in the same small groups, aspects of their host culture that they have noticed. If this course takes place in the participants' home country, replace "host culture" with American culture or another culture.

5. Put out materials for a collage, such as construction paper, scissors, glue, magazines, and markers.

6. Ask participants to divide the paper in half.

7. Let them know that they are going to make a collage.

8. Explain that one half of the collage will depict the similarities that they observed, both culturally and personally. The other half will depict differences that they observed, both culturally and personally. Encourage participants to include personal observations as well as cultural observations.

9. Let participants know that they will be sharing their collages with the rest of the group. Note: It is nice to play music in English in the background while participants work. Feel free to let participants make requests. YouTube.com is a wonderful resource for this.

10. When participants are done, have everyone sit in a circle and ask participants to share their collages.
11. Conclude this activity with a closing reflection.
    a. What did you learn about culture?
    b. What did you learn about one another?
    c. Is it helpful to explore cultural similarities and differences? Why or why not?

Conclusion

Plant the seeds of peace, joy, and understanding
in yourself in order to facilitate the work of
transformation in the depths of your consciousness.

—*THICH NHAT HANH*

*B*REATHE is a guide for living a happier, more mindful life. The principles discussed—mindfulness, nonjudgment, compassion, acceptance, gratitude, generosity, love, joy, and understanding—are applicable in our personal and professional lives. It is my hope that the practice of these principles leads to a more integrated and holistic approach to work and to life. When we bring these practices into our professional space, our participants feel safe to explore and learn without judgment, blame, or criticism. This is true when we apply these principles to our personal lives as well. When everything we do and every person we encounter is experienced through the lens of nonjudgment and mindful attention, we are on a path to greater well-being and inner peace.

Breath is the starting point to mindfulness. When we remember to breathe consciously, we become aware of our body. When we become aware of our body, we begin to pay attention. When we pay attention, without judgment, we are practicing mindfulness. Meditation is a good place to begin the practice of mindfulness. It provides the time and space for quiet, observant reflection. With time, we are able to extend those moments of mindfulness beyond meditation into our daily lives. As we practice mindfulness more, we begin to notice the moments when we are not being mindful, and those moments of judgment become fewer.

Reflection is a part of the process that promotes greater mindfulness and awareness. Reflection is a process of observation. When we observe our thoughts, actions, sensations, and feelings with mindfulness and nonjudgment, we become aware of the underlying reasons for those thoughts, actions, sensations, and feelings. This, in turn, leads us on the path toward continual growth and improvement.

Empathy is our emotional connection to others. Compassion is working with these connections in order to help others. Compassion is the foundation for integrating acts of kindness into our lives and the lives of others. Once we realize that all human beings experience suffering and all human beings want to be happy, we have uncovered the common bond that connects all of us to one another. The ultimate goal of our existence, then, is to alleviate suffering for ourselves and others, and to contribute to our well-being and the well-being of others. Mindfulness and reflection are important components here as well. As we pay attention without judgment and observe suffering, we begin to explore ways to diminish that suffering and increase well-being.

Acceptance also requires the practice of mindfulness and nonjudgment. In addition, it requires the absence of blame and criticism. "Grant me the serenity to accept the things I cannot change" (Niebuhr, 1987, p. 251). When we are able to accept situations as they are, and not as we wish them to be, free from judgment, we are able to feel more peaceful. When we feel more peaceful, we are able to release feelings of negativity. This ultimately "allows us to experience the joyful gift of forgiveness" (p. 38).

Thankfulness is another type of gift; it is a gift to ourselves and to the recipient. When we practice gratitude regularly in our lives, our physical, emotional, and social well-being improve. We *feel* better about ourselves when we remember to be grateful. Observing the natural world is a good place to start to look for reasons to be grateful. Each day is different than the previous day, even if those differences are quite subtle. Gratitude can be cultivated, even when gratitude doesn't come naturally to us. If we think of just one new thing each day to be grateful for, we train our brain to look for *more* instances of gratitude in our lives (Borysenko, 2014). This is the miracle of the neuroplasticity of our brains. For those of us who may be having trouble thinking of anything to be grateful for, neuroplasticity is a good reason to feel grateful!

Hearten brings joy and love into the world. When we give from our hearts with love and joy, we are contributing to the well-being of ourselves and others. Love is the universal emotion from which all other positive emotions arise. These positive emotions include nonjudgment, compassion, acceptance, forgiveness, gratitude, and generosity. "When we practice [these positive emotions] as part of our daily lives, we are incorporating 'heart' into everything we experience. This is the essence of love" (p. 51), and I hope this has been the essence of this book as well.

Engaging with others is about connection. Humans are hardwired to connect with one another as a result of the limbic region of our brain (Siegel, 2011, p. 17). We live in an interconnected world. This interconnectedness extends beyond our human relationships into the natural world. When we realize this, we realize how our actions also extend far beyond ourselves. When we perform acts of kindness, we contribute positively to the health and well-being of ourselves, all human beings, and the planet.

Understanding is the final contribution to our web of well-being. It integrates mindfulness, nonjudgment, acceptance, compassion, and awareness to create a deeper level of connection. The key to understanding is communication. This communication isn't about being right or wrong or giving advice; this communication is about listening and being present for another person. Communication is about mindfulness and giving our undivided attention to others in order to help them to help themselves. Understanding may be extended beyond individual interpersonal relationships to include groups, cultures, and countries. When we explore our relationships with the goal of understanding, we move toward achieving greater harmony and peace.

A natural outgrowth of experiencing life with mindfulness, nonjudgment, compassion, acceptance, gratitude, generosity, love, and understanding is a feeling of well-being. True well-being brings with it a sense of equanimity and inner peace. This becomes a part of everything we do. Our participants feel our nonjudgment, compassion, acceptance and love, which create more of the same as well as a sense of safety and comfort in the workplace and classroom. Our friends and family feel it and respond more openly. Our colleagues feel it and work more cooperatively. I leave you with one last meditation that promotes a feeling of equanimity. I wish you all the absence of suffering in all its guises, and the presence of love, balance, and inner peace in your life.

You may say I'm a dreamer, but I'm not the only one. I
hope someday you'll join us. And the world will live as one.

—JOHN LENNON

Equanimity Meditation

This meditation is adopted from Jack Kornfield's "Meditation on Equanimity" from his book *A Path With Heart* (1993, p. 331). As with all activities, feel free to modify it for your participants' (and your) needs.

This meditation activity is divided into three parts. The introduction familiarizes participants with the topic, including new vocabulary. The listening phase includes the actual listening portion. The post phase is the opportunity to reflect on the activity, including the exploration of next steps.

Goal: to experience a sense of peacefulness.

Introduction:

1. Before beginning this meditation, ask the participants to notice how they are feeling, physically and mentally. Ask them to share with a partner or with the whole group.
2. Write the word "equanimity" on the board.
3. Ask participants what the word means.
4. Ask for synonyms, such as balance, peace, tranquility, quiet, calm.
5. Ask them to share with a partner a time when they felt peaceful.
6. See if anyone would like to share with the whole group.
7. If you have done the self-compassion meditation on pages 25–28 or the loving-kindness meditation on pages 56–60 with the whole group, review those meditations before moving on to the equanimity meditation.
   a. What do you remember about the meditations?
   b. What was the main theme of the meditations?

    c. What was important for you about the meditations?

    d. Where is your third eye? What does it represent?

8. Review the phrases in the meditation:

    a. May I feel safe and peaceful.

    b. May I be accepting of myself and others.

    c. May I learn to see the rising and passing of all nature and life with equanimity and balance.

    d. May I bring compassion and equanimity into the events of the world.

Listening Phase:

In the during phase, you may read or play a recording of the following. The recording of this meditation is available at http://vocaroo.com/i/s1Q178IOipVH.

[Begin Meditation]

This is a meditation that focuses on equanimity. Equanimity is a feeling of peacefulness. Equanimity gives us time and space for quiet meditation. Equanimity allows us to open our hearts and let loving-kindness flow from within.

Find a comfortable position. You may sit in a chair or on the floor. If you sit in a chair, try to keep your feet flat on the floor or in a cross-legged position. If you sit on the floor, you may sit on a pillow for comfort. Also, try to sit in a comfortable cross-legged position. Keep your back straight and shoulders broad. Place your hands in your lap or on your thighs, palms facing up in a relaxed position.

Gently close your eyes. Your gaze may be toward the floor or toward your third eye. (Your third eye is located about one inch above and between your eyes.)

Notice any tension you may feel in your body. Try to relax any areas of tension that you notice.

Now begin to notice your breath. As you breathe, try to release any disturbing thoughts or feelings. When you inhale, notice how the breath feels entering through the nostrils, and then feel your diaphragm as it expands. Now exhale and release the breath. Notice how it feels when your diaphragm contracts and the air exits through your nostrils. Repeat this three times.

When thoughts arise, simply notice them with acceptance and without criticism and judgment, and return to the focus on your breath. Enjoy this opportunity to sit quietly.

When we feel equanimity, we feel peaceful. Equanimity can be practiced and learned just as we have been practicing nonjudgment, compassion, and loving-kindness. We all have lessons to learn and, while we may try to help, there may times that we cannot change things. We all must learn in our own way and on our own path.

Now begin to reflect on the benefit of a mind that has balance and equanimity. Think about what a gift it can be to bring a peaceful heart to the world around you. Let yourself feel an inner sense of balance and ease. As you do this, continue to take deep, slow breaths.

Begin repeating this phrase to yourself:
May I feel balanced and peaceful.
May I feel balanced and peaceful.
May I feel balanced and peaceful.

We must all learn in our own way and on our own path.

Repeat this phrase to yourself:
May I be accepting of myself and others.
May I be accepting of myself and others.
May I be accepting of myself and others.

Part of achieving a sense of equanimity is realizing that not everything is in our control. As we acknowledge this, repeat this phrase to yourself:
May I learn to see the rising and passing of all nature and life with equanimity and balance.
May I learn to see the rising and passing of all nature and life with equanimity and balance.
May I learn to see the rising and passing of all nature and life with equanimity and balance.

Even when we are kind and compassionate, there may be circumstances and events that we cannot change. However, we may continue to bring compassion into the world.

Repeat this phrase to yourself:
May I bring compassion and equanimity into the events of the world.

May I bring compassion and equanimity into the events of the world.
May I bring compassion and equanimity into the events of the world.

In closing, repeat this phrase:
May I experience all life with balance and equanimity.
May I experience all life with balance and equanimity.
May I experience all life with balance and equanimity.

We will now conclude this equanimity meditation. As you continue with your day, remember, if possible, a moment of peace or equanimity that you experienced during this meditation. As you go through the day, repeat this phrase: May I feel balanced and peaceful.

We will conclude this meditation by sending peace, balance, equanimity, compassion, healing, happiness, and love to ourselves and everyone.
[End Meditation]

Post Phase:
The post phase is the opportunity for reflection. Discussion may include any combination of writing, reading, speaking, and listening individually, in pairs, small groups, or with the whole group.

1. Here are some possible questions:
    a. What did you think of this meditation?
    b. Were you comfortable with the phrases that you repeated?
    c. What happened when you had thoughts?
    d. Do you feel different after meditating? Why or why not?

    e. What are the differences that you notice?

    f. Is equanimity important to you? Why or why not?

2. Have participants stand or sit in a circle and ask them to share how they are feeling.

Appendix

Important concepts and vocabulary from *Nonviolent Communication* (Rosenberg, 2003, pp. 209–210).

The Four-Part Nonviolent Communication Process

Clearly expressing how *I am* without blaming or criticizing.

Listening to how *you are* without hearing blame or criticism.

Observations

What I/you observe (see, hear, remember, imagine, free from my evaluations) that does or does not contribute to my/your well-being.

"When I/you (see, hear)…"

Feelings

How I/you feel (emotion or sensation rather than thought) in relation to what I/you observe:

"I/you feel..."

Needs

What I/you need or value that causes my feelings:

"...because I/you need/value..."

Requests

Clearly requesting that which would enrich my/your life without demanding.

The concrete actions I/you would like taken:

"Would you be willing to..."

Some Basic Feelings We All Have

When needs are fulfilled:
amazed, comfortable, confident, eager, energetic, fulfilled, glad, hopeful, inspired, intrigued, joyous, moved, optimistic, proud, relieved, stimulated, surprised, thankful, touched, trustful

When needs are not fulfilled:
angry, annoyed, concerned, confused, disappointed, discouraged, distressed, embarrassed, frustrated, helpless, hopeless,

impatient, irritated, lonely, nervous, overwhelmed, puzzled, re-
luctant, sad, uncomfortable

Some Basic Needs We All Have

Autonomy:
choosing dreams, goals, values
choosing plans for fulfilling one's dreams, goals, values

Celebration:
celebrating the creation of life and dreams fulfilled
celebrating lives of loved ones, dreams, and more

Integrity:
authenticity, creativity, meaning, self-worth

Interdependence:
acceptance, appreciation, closeness, community, contribution to
the enrichment of life, emotional safety, love, honesty, respect,
support, understanding, trust

Physical Nurturance:
air, food, water, movement, exercise, rest, protection

Play:
fun, laughter

Spiritual Communion:
beauty, harmony, inspiration, order, peace

References

Barduhn, S. (1998). *Traits and conditions that accelerate teacher learning* (Unpublished doctoral dissertation). Thames Valley University. Retrieved from http://works.bepress.com/susan_barduhn/26

Berk, L. (2012). Laughter Online University. Retrieved from http://www.healinglaughter.org/blog/tag/loma-linda-university/

Borysenko, J. (2014). I can do it [Keynote]. Denver, CO: Hay House.

Chopra, D. (1994). *The seven spiritual laws of success*. Novato, CA: New World Library.

Chopra, D. (2014). Feeling love [Weblog post]. Retrieved from https://www.deepakchopra.com/blog/article/4676

Chopra, D. (2014). Spiritual solutions [Keynote]. Carlsbad, CA: The Chopra Center.

Chopra, D. (2015). The benefits of meditation. Retrieved from https://chopra.com/ccl/why-meditate-0

Chopra, D., & Simon, D. (2004). *The seven spiritual laws of yoga: A practical guide to healing body, mind, and spirit*. Hoboken, NJ: Wiley.

Clift, R. T., Houston, W. R., & Pugach, M. C. (Eds.). (1990). *Encouraging reflective practice in education: An analysis of issues and programs*. New York, NY: Teachers College Press.

Covey, S. R. (1989). *The 7 habits of highly effective people: Powerful lessons in personal change*. New York: Simon & Schuster.

Curran, C. A. (1978). *Understanding: An essential ingredient in human belonging*. East Dubuque, IL: Counseling-learning Publications.

Dalai Lama XIV. (2012). *Beyond religion*. New York, NY: Mariner Books.

Decety, J. (2010, December). The neurodevelopment of empathy in humans. Retrieved from http://www.ncbi.nlm.nih.gov/pmc/articles/PMC3021497/

Dewey, J. (2012). *How we think*. Renaissance Classics.

Edwards, G. (2006). *Wild love*. London: Piatkus.

Einstein, A. (1931). From a speech to the New History Society (14 December 1930), reprinted in Militant pacifism. In *Cosmic religion*. New York, NY: Covici-Friede.

Emmons, R. (2010). Why gratitude is good. Retrieved from http://greatergood.berkeley.edu/article/item/why_gratitude_is_good/

Emmons, R. (2010). *Greater Good Gratitude Summit*. Retrieved from https://www.youtube.com/watch?v=6Fdfz2tbxJU#t=78

Emmons, R. (2013). How gratitude can help you through hard times. Retrieved from http://greatergood.berkeley.edu/article/item/how_gratitude_can_help_you_through_hard_times

Goleman, D., Bennett, L., & Barlow, Z. (2013). Five ways to develop "ecoliteracy." Retrieved from http://greatergood.berkeley.edu/article/item/five_ways_to_develop_ecoliteracy

Hanh, T. N. (1991). *Peace is every step*. New York, NY: Bantam Books.

Heubeck, E. (2006). Boost your health with a dose of gratitude. Retrieved from http://www.webmd.com/women/features/gratitude-health-boost

Holden, R. (2013). *Loveability: Knowing how to love and be loved.* Carlsbad, CA: Hay House.

Israel, I. (2013, May 30). What are the differences between mindfulness, mindfulness meditation, and meditation? Retrieved from http://www. huffingtonpost.com/ira-israel/types-of-mindfulness_b_3347428. html

James, W. (1983). *The principles of psychology.* Cambridge, MA: Harvard University Press.

Kabat-Zinn, J. (1994). *Wherever you go, there you are.* New York, NY: Hyperion Books.

Kataria, M. (2011). 5 day certified laughter yoga teacher training (CLYT). Interlakken, Switzerland.

Kataria, M. (2015). 5 day certified laughter yoga teacher training (CLYT). Retrieved from www.laughteryoga.org.

Kolb, D. A. (1984). *Experiential learning: Experience as the source of learning and Development.* Englewood Cliffs, NJ: Prentice Hall.

Kornfield, J. (1993). *A path with heart.* New York, NY: Bantam Books.

Leuras-Tramma, N. (2011). Feeling connected makes us kind. Retrieved from http://greatergood.berkeley.edu/article/item/feeling_ connected_makes_us_kind

Lyubomirsky, S. (2010). Happiness for a lifetime. Retrieved from http:// greatergood.berkeley.edu/article/item/happiness_for_a_lifetime/

Lyubomirsky, S., Sheldon, K. M., & Schkade, D. (2005). Pursuing happiness: The architecture of sustainable change for a lifetime. *Review of General Psychology, 9*(2), 111–132. doi:10.1037/1089-2680.9.2.111

Marsh, J., & Suttie, J. (2010). 5 ways giving is good for you. Retrieved from http://greatergood.berkeley.edu/article/item/5_ways_giving_ is_good_for_you

McGreevey, S. (January 21, 2011). Eight weeks to a better brain. *Harvard Gazette.* Retrieved from http://news.harvard.edu/gazette/ story/2011/01/eight-weeks-to-a-better-brain/

Moll, J., Krueger, F., Zahn, R., Pardini, M., Oliveira-Souza, R., Grafman, J. (2006). Human fronto-mesolimbic networks guide decisions about charitable donation. *Proceedings of the National Academy of Sciences of the United States of America, 103*, 15623–15628.

Moran, P. (2001). *Teaching culture*. Boston, MA: Heinle Cengage Learning.

Morin, A. (2014, November 23). 7 scientifically proven benefits of gratitude that will motivate you to give thanks year-round. Retrieved from http://www.forbes.com/sites/amymorin/2014/11/23/7-scientifically-proven-benefits-of-gratitude-that-will-motivate-you

Negi, G. L. (2015). *Cognitively-based compassion training*. Atlanta, GA: Emory University.

Niebuhr, R. (1987). *Essential Reinhold Niebuhr: Selected essays and addresses* (R. M. Brown, Ed.). New Haven, CT: Yale University Press, New Ed edition.

Oman, D., Thoresen, C. E., & McMahon, K. (1999). Volunteerism and Mortality among the Community-dwelling Elderly. *Journal of Health Psychology, 4*(3), 301–316. doi:10.1177/135910539900400301

Passarelli, M. A., & Kolb, D. A. (2012). Using experiential learning theory to promote participant learning and development in programs of education abroad. In M. Vande Berg, M. Page, & K. Lou (Eds.), *Participant learning abroad*. Sterling, VA: PDF.

Post, S. G. (2005). Altruism, happiness, and health: It's good to be good. *International Journal of Behavioral Medicine, 12*(2), 66–77. doi:10.1207/s15327558ijbm1202_4

Robbins, T. (2003). *Unlimited power: The science of personal achievement*. New York, NY: Free Press.

Rosenberg, M. B. (2003). *Nonviolent communication: A language of compassion*. Encinitas, CA: PuddleDancer Press.

Salzberg, S. (1995). *Lovingkindness: The revolutionary art of happiness*. Boston, MA: Shambhala Classics.

Schön, D. A. (1983). *The Reflective Practitioner: How Professionals Think in Action.* New York, NY: Basic Books.

Schwartzberg, L. (2011). Nature. Beauty. Gratitude. Retrieved from http://www.ted.com/talks/louie_schwartzberg_nature_beauty_gratitude?language=en

Seppälä, E. (2013, September 11). 20 scientific reasons to start meditating today. Retrieved from https://www.psychologytoday.com/blog/feeling-it/201309/20-scientific-reasons-start-meditating-today

Siegel, D. J. (2011). *Mindsight: Change your brain and your life.* New York, NY: Bantam Books.

Smith, M. K. (2011). Retrieved from https://www.andrew.cmu.edu/user/skey/research_prev/reading/reflection_educational_role/et-Schön.htm

Steindl-Rast, D. (2013). Want to be happy? Be grateful. Retrieved from https://www.ted.com/talks/david_steindl_rast_want_to_be_happy_be_grateful#t-134986

Swisa, M. (2013). *Positive attitude handbook.* Santa Fe, NM: Green Back Publishing, LLC.

Tolle, E. (1999). *The power of now: A guide to spiritual enlightenment.* Novato, CA: New World Library.

Tolle, E. (1999). *The power of now: A guide to spiritual enlightenment.* Novato, CA: New World Library.

Tremmel, R. (1993). Zen and the Art of Reflective Practice in Teacher Education. *Harvard Educational Review, 63*(4), 434–459. doi:10.17763/haer.63.4.m42704n778561176

Tsu, L. (1972). *Lao-Tsu: Tao Te Ching* (G. Feng & J. English, Eds.). New York, NY: Random House.

Unknown. (2012). Fundamentals of Buddhism. Retrieved from http://www.buddhanet.net/fundbud4.htm

Unknown. *Definition of reflect.* Retrieved from https://www.google.com/search?q=definition+of+reflect&ie=utf-8&oe=utf-8

Unknown. (2015). *Greek words for love.* Retrieved from http://en.wikipedia. org/wiki/Greek_words_for_love.

Yeganeh, B., & Kolb, D. (2009). Mindfulness and experiential learning. *OD Practitioner, 41*(3).

About the Author

Maxine Swisa used to be a top-level executive at a Fortune 1000 company. She was successful, but she wasn't happy. Swisa soon realized that this wasn't the life she wanted.

Swisa changed her path and began helping others find comfort, peace, and joy in their lives. Her unique curriculum, BREATHE, utilizes research into neuroplasticity and positive psychology to teach mindfulness and improve interpersonal relationship skills. Her workshops help hundreds of people find compassion, self-acceptance, and happiness.

When Swisa isn't teaching, writing, or developing new coursework, she is spending time with her two daughters, hiking, meditating, practicing yoga, meeting new people, and traveling. She hails from Santa Fe, New Mexico, the Land of Enchantment.